VOLUME I

CHAPTERS 1-14

WORKING PAPERS
FOR USE WITH

FUNDAMENTAL

ACCOUNTING

PRINCIPLES

TWELFTH EDITION

KERMIT D. LARSON
THE UNIVERSITY OF TEXAS AT AUSTIN

IRWIN
HOMEWOOD, IL 60430
BOSTON, MA 02116

© Richard D. Irwin, Inc., 1987 and 1990

Printed in the United States of America.

ISBN 0-256-08063-1

5 6 7 8 9 0 VK 6 5 4 3 2

Contents

PROBLEM 1-1 or 1-1A

Name _____

	ASSETS				=	LIABILITIES		+	OWNER'S EQUITY	
CASH	+ ACCOUNTS RECEIVABLE	+ OFFICE SUPPLIES	+ OFFICE EQUIPMENT	+ BUILDING	= ACCOUNTS PAYABLE	+ NOTES PAYABLE		+ CAROL OLDS, CAPITAL	EXPLANATION
$40,000								$40,000	Investment
−35,000				100,000		65,000			
Bal $5,000				100,000		65,000			
			500		65,000	65,000	Bal	$500	Investment
								40,500	
Bal $5,000		+350	500	100,000		65,000		$40,500	Bal
−350		350							
								40,500	
Bal 4650		350	+6000	100,000	6,000	65,000		40,500	
+530		350	6500	100,000	6,000	65,000		+530	Revenue
Bal 5180		350	6500	100,000	6,000	65,000		41,030	
−160			6500	100,000	6,000	65,000		−160	Expense
Bal 5020		350	6500	100,000	6,000	65,000		40,870	
+900	+900	350	6500	100,000	6,000	65,000		+900	Revenue
Bal 5020	900	350	6500	100,000	6,000	65,000		41,770	
−600	−600	350	6500	100,000	−600	65,000		41,770	
Bal 4420	300	350	6500	100,000	5400	65,000		41,770	
+600									
5020	300	350	6500	100,000	5400	65,000		41,770	
−550								655−	Expense
Bal 4470	300	350	6500	100,000	5400	65,000		(225)4	
−300								−300	Withdraw
Bal 4170	300	350	6500	100,000	5400	65,000		40,920	

PROBLEM 1-2 or 1-2A

Name _____

		ASSETS				= LIABILITIES +	OWNER'S EQUITY	
DATE	CASH	+ ACCOUNTS RECEIVABLE	+ OFFICE SUPPLIES	+ LAW LIBRARY	+ OFFICE EQUIPMENT	= ACCOUNTS PAYABLE	+ GARY MEYER, CAPITAL	EXPLANATION
May 1	$6000						$6000	Investment
	– 1000						– 1000	Expense
Bal	5000						5000	
	– 2000			+ 4000		+ 2000		
Bal	3000			4000		2000	5000	
May 2	– 200		+ 200					
i	2800		200	4000		2000	5000	
May 7	+ 680						+ 680	Revenue

Part 1

Part 2

PROBLEM 1-4 or 1-4A

Name _____

	ASSETS				= LIABILITIES =	+ OWNER'S EQUITY +	
DATE	CASH	+ ACCOUNTS RECEIVABLE +	PREPAID INSURANCE +	DRAFTING SUPPLIES	ACCOUNTS PAYABLE	HANK SETA, CAPITAL	EXPLANATION
June 1	4500					4500	Investment
	-900					-900	Expense
	3600					3600	
	-115			+115			
	3485			115		3600	Expense
	-150			115		-150	
	3335			115		3450	Revenue
	+375			115		+375	Revenue
	3710	+1150		115		3825	Expense
		1150		115		+1150	
	3710	1150		115		4975	Revenue
	-750	-1150		115		-750	
	2960	0		115		4225	Revenue
	+1150	+1200		115		4225	Expense
	4110	1200		115		+1200	
	4110	1200		115	+100	5425	Revenue
June 22	4110	1200		+100	100	5425	Expense
24	4110	+900		215	100	+900	
	4110	2100		215	100	6325	Revenue
	+1200	2100		215	+140	-140	Expense
	5310	-1200		215	240	6185	
	-100	900		215	-100		
	5210	900		215	140	5815	Expense
	-135	900		215	140	-135	Expense
	5075	600		215	140	5090	Expense
	4980	600		215	140	5155	

Part 1 _____

_____

_____

_____

_____

_____

_____

_____

_____

_____

_____

_____

_____

_____

_____

_____

_____

_____

_____

_____

_____

Part 2

Part 3

Part 4

Part 5

Cash

(a)	42000	(b)	35000
(g)	8500	(f)	600
(m)	210	(k)	150
		(i)	60
	11960	(f)	840
		(e)	600
		(n)	1500

Accounts Payable

(i)	60	(c)	60
		(e)	720
			720

Notes Payable

(b)	100000

Accounts Receivable

(k)	210	(m)	210

Carol Blake, Capital

		(a)	48000
		(d)	7200
			55200

Office Supplies

(c)	60

Carol Blake, Withdrawals

(n)	1500

Office Equipment

(a)	6000	(f)	140
(e)	720		
(f)	980		
	7560		

Commissions Earned

(g)	8500

Automobile

(d)	7200

Appraisal Fees Earned

(k)	210

Land

(b)	30000

Office Salaries Expense

(f)	600
(e)	600
	1200

Building

(b)	105000

C.

Advertising Expense

(k)	150

Carol Blake
Trial Balance
2/2/93

Cash	$11960	
Office Supply	60	
Office Equipment	7560	
Automobile	7200	
Land	30000	
Building	105000	
Acct Payable		$720
Note Payable		100000
Carol, Blake, capital		55200
Carol withdraw	1500	
Commission Earned		8500
Appraisal Fee Earned		210
Office Salary Expense	1200	
Advertising Expense	150	
Total	$164630	$164630

GENERAL JOURNAL   PAGE 1

DATE	ACCOUNT TITLES AND EXPLANATION	P.R.	DEBIT	CREDIT

GENERAL JOURNAL

DATE	ACCOUNT TITLES AND EXPLANATION	P.R.	DEBIT	CREDIT

GENERAL LEDGER

Cash   ACCT. NO. 111

DATE	EXPLANATION	P.R.	DEBIT	CREDIT	BALANCE

Accounts Receivable   ACCT. NO. 117

DATE	EXPLANATION	P.R.	DEBIT	CREDIT	BALANCE

Office Supplies   ACCT. NO. 131

DATE	EXPLANATION	P.R.	DEBIT	CREDIT	BALANCE

Prepaid Insurance   ACCT. NO. 133

DATE	EXPLANATION	P.R.	DEBIT	CREDIT	BALANCE

Prepaid Rent
ACCT. NO. 134

DATE	EXPLANATION	P.R.	DEBIT	CREDIT	BALANCE

Office Equipment
ACCT. NO. 156

DATE	EXPLANATION	P.R.	DEBIT	CREDIT	BALANCE

Accounts Payable
ACCT. NO. 211

DATE	EXPLANATION	P.R.	DEBIT	CREDIT	BALANCE

Jack Fish, Capital
ACCT. NO. 311

DATE	EXPLANATION	P.R.	DEBIT	CREDIT	BALANCE

Jack Fish, Withdrawals
ACCT. NO. 316

DATE	EXPLANATION	P.R.	DEBIT	CREDIT	BALANCE

Accounting Fees Earned   ACCT. NO. 412

DATE		EXPLANATION	P.R.	DEBIT	CREDIT	BALANCE

Utilities Expense   ACCT. NO. 651

DATE		EXPLANATION	P.R.	DEBIT	CREDIT	BALANCE

Cash

Land

Accounts Payable

Notes Payable

Accounts Receivable

Wayne Seale, Capital

Prepaid Insurance

Wayne Seale, Withdrawals

Office Equipment

Excavating Revenue

Machinery

Machinery Repairs Expense

Building

Wages Expense

Machinery Rentals Expense   **Gas and Oil Expense**

CHAPTER 2   **PROBLEM 2-4 or 2-4A**   Name _____

DATE	ACCOUNT TITLES AND EXPLANATION	P.R.	DEBIT	CREDIT

DATE	ACCOUNT TITLES AND EXPLANATION	P.R.	DEBIT	CREDIT

GENERAL LEDGER

Cash ACCT. NO. 111

DATE	EXPLANATION	P.R.	DEBIT	CREDIT	BALANCE
			7500		
				1500	
				1125	
				265	
8			785		
12				720	
15				825	
21				230	
27			1800		
28				300	
31				825	
31				120	
31				200	3975

Accounts Receivable ACCT. NO. 112

DATE	EXPLANATION	P.R.	DEBIT	CREDIT	BALANCE
17			1800		
25			1800		
27				1800	
					1800

Prepaid Rent ACCT. NO. 113

DATE	EXPLANATION	P.R.	DEBIT	CREDIT	BALANCE
			1500		

Prepaid Insurance ACCT. NO. 114

DATE	EXPLANATION	P.R.	DEBIT	CREDIT	BALANCE
12			720		

Drafting Supplies   ACCT. NO. 11☐

DATE		EXPLANATION	P.R.	DEBIT	CREDIT	BALANCE
				7 1 2 5		
				2 6 5		
	14			5 5		
						3 2 0

Office and Drafting Equipment   ACCT. NO. 131

DATE		EXPLANATION	P.R.	DEBIT	CREDIT	BALANCE
				7 1 2 5		
				1 7 5		
						7 3 0 0

Accounts Payable   ACCT. NO. 211

DATE		EXPLANATION	P.R.	DEBIT	CREDIT	BALANCE
	14				6 0 0 0	
	21				2 3 0	
				2 3 0		
						6 0 0 0

Paula Hill, Capital   ACCT. NO. 311

DATE		EXPLANATION	P.R.	DEBIT	CREDIT	BALANCE
					7 5 0 0	

Paula Hill, Withdrawals   ACCT. NO. 312

DATE		EXPLANATION	P.R.	DEBIT	CREDIT	BALANCE
	28			3 0 0		

Architectural Fees Earned   ACCT. NO. 411

DATE	EXPLANATION	P.R.	DEBIT	CREDIT	BALANCE
				7 8 5	
17				1 8 0 0	
25				1 8 0 0	
				4 3 8 5	

Salaries Expense   ACCT. NO. 511

DATE	EXPLANATION	P.R.	DEBIT	CREDIT	BALANCE
			8 2 5		
31			8 2 5		
			1 6 5 0		

Blueprinting Expense   ACCT. NO. 512

DATE	EXPLANATION	P.R.	DEBIT	CREDIT	BALANCE
31			2 0 0		

Utilities Expense   ACCT. NO. 513

DATE	EXPLANATION	P.R.	DEBIT	CREDIT	BALANCE
31			1 2 0		

$$\underline{A} \quad = \quad \underline{L} \qquad \underline{OE}$$

$$15615 \qquad\qquad 6000 \qquad 9615$$

PH Arch.
Trial Balance

May 31, 1933

GENERAL JOURNAL

DATE	ACCOUNT TITLES AND EXPLANATION	P.R.	DEBIT	CREDIT
1993 APR 1	Cash		3000	
	Law Library		1500	
	Amy Tuck, Capital			4500
	Owner's Investment			
1	Rent Expense		600	
	Cash			600
	Rent Expense for April			
1	Insurance Expense		45	
	Cash			45
	Insurance Expense .			
3	Office Supplies		50	
	Accounts Payable .			50
	Purchase of office supplies on Credit			
9	Cash		300	
	Legal Fee Earned			300
	Payment Revenue .			
13	Account Payable		50	
	Cash			50
	Pay for Office supplies purchased on April 3			
16	Account Receivable		1000	
	Legal Fee Earned .			1000
	Revenue .			
23	Account Receivable		900	
	Legal Fee Earned			900
	Revenue			
26	Cash		1000	
	Account Receivable			1000
	Payment of Legal Fee			
28	Owner's Withdraw		20	
	Cash			20
	Withdraw .			
29	Office Supplies		54	
	Account Payable			54
	Purchase office supplies on Credit .			

DATE		ACCOUNT TITLES AND EXPLANATION	P.R.	DEBIT	CREDIT
	30	Telephone Expense		30	
		Cash			30
		Expense			
				1150	
	30	Salaries Expense			1150
		Cash			
		salaries Expense .			
	30	Prepaid Rent		1200	
		Cash			1200
		Prepayment of Rent for June, May			
	30	Prepaid Insurance		495	
		Cash			495
		Prepayment of insurance premium of			
		the next 11 months			

Cash   ACCT. NO. 111

DATE		EXPLANATION	P.R.	DEBIT	CREDIT	BALANCE
1993 Aug	1			3000		3000
	1				600	2400
	1				45	2355
	9			300		2655
	13				50	2605
	26			1000		3605
	28				20	3585
	30				30	3555
	30				1150	2405
	30				1200	1205
	30				495	710

Accounts Receivable   ACCT. NO. 112

DATE		EXPLANATION	P.R.	DEBIT	CREDIT	BALANCE
1993 Apr	16			1000		1000
	23			900		1900
	26				1000	900

Prepaid Rent   ACCT. NO. 113

DATE		EXPLANATION	P.R.	DEBIT	CREDIT	BALANCE
1993 Apr	30			1200		1200

Prepaid Insurance   ACCT. NO. 114

DATE		EXPLANATION	P.R.	DEBIT	CREDIT	BALANCE
1993 Apr	30			495		495

Office Supplies   ACCT. NO. 115

DATE	EXPLANATION	P.R.	DEBIT	CREDIT	BALANCE
1993 Apr 3			50		50
29			54		104

Law Library   ACCT. NO. 131

DATE	EXPLANATION	P.R.	DEBIT	CREDIT	BALANCE
1993 Apr 1			1500		1500

Accounts Payable   ACCT. NO. 211

DATE	EXPLANATION	P.R.	DEBIT	CREDIT	BALANCE
1993 Apr 3				50	50
13			50		0
29				54	54

Amy Tuck, Capital   ACCT. NO. 311

DATE	EXPLANATION	P.R.	DEBIT	CREDIT	BALANCE
1993 Apr				4500	4500

Amy Tuck, Withdrawals   ACCT. NO. 312

DATE	EXPLANATION	P.R.	DEBIT	CREDIT	BALANCE
1993 Apr 28			20		

Legal Fees Earned   ACCT. NO. 411

DATE		EXPLANATION	P.R.	DEBIT	CREDIT	BALANCE
1993 Apr	9				300	300
	16				1000	1300
	23				900	2200

Rent Expense   ACCT. NO. 511

DATE		EXPLANATION	P.R.	DEBIT	CREDIT	BALANCE
1993 Apr	1			600		600

Salaries Expense   ACCT. NO. 512

DATE		EXPLANATION	P.R.	DEBIT	CREDIT	BALANCE
1993 Apr	30			1150		1150

Telephone Expense   ACCT. NO. 513

DATE		EXPLANATION	P.R.	DEBIT	CREDIT	BALANCE
1993 Apr	30			30		30

Insurance Expense   ACCT. NO. 514

DATE		EXPLANATION	P.R.	DEBIT	CREDIT	BALANCE
1993 Apr	1			45		45

Amy Tuck, Attorney
Trial Balance
April 30, 1993

Cash	$710	
Account Receivable	900	
Prepaid Rent	1200	
Prepaid Insurance	495	
Office Supplies	104	
Law Library	1500	
Account Payable		$54
Amy Tuck, Capital		4500
Amy Tuck, Withdrew	20	
Legal Fee Earned		2200
Rent Expense	600	
Salaries Expense	1150	
Telephone Expense	30	
Insurance Expense	45	
	$6754	$6754

Amy Tuck, Attorney
Income Statement
For Month Ended April 30, 1993

Revenue :			
Legal fees Earned			$2200
Operating Expenses :			
Rent Expenses	$600		
Salaries Expenses	1150		
Telephone Expenses	30		
Insurance Expenses	45		
		1825	
Total Operating Expenses			
Net Income			$375

Amy Tuck, Attorney.
Statement of Changes in Owner's
Equity For Month Ended April 30, 1993

Amy Tuck, Capital March 31, 1993			-0-
Plus: Investment by Owner.	4500		
Net Income	375	4875	
Total		$4875	
Less Withdraw by Owner.		20	
Amy Tuck, Capital, April 30, 1993		$4855	

Amy Tuck, Attorney.
Balance Sheet
Assets   April 30, 1993

Assets			Liabilities		
Cash	$710				
Account Receivable.	900		Accounts Payable	$54	
Prepaid Rent	1200				
Prepaid Insurance	495		Owner's Equity		
Office Supplies	104				
Law Library	1500		Amy Tuck, Capital	4855	
Total Assets	$4909		Total Liabilities and	$4909	
			Owner's Equity		

Part 1

GENERAL JOURNAL

DATE		ACCOUNT TITLES AND EXPLANATION	P.R.	DEBIT	CREDIT
Dec	31	Office supplies Expense		835	
		Office supplies			835
Dec	31	Insurance Expense		1140	
		Prepaid Insurance			1140
		$1260 \div 3 = 420$			
		$810 \div 2 \times \frac{8}{12} = 270$			
		$600 \times \frac{9}{12} = 450$			
Dec	31	Salaries Expense		270	
		Salaries Payable			270
		$(60+75) \times 2 =$			
Dec	31	Depreciation Expense, building		13500	
		Accumulated Depreciation Building			13500
		$675000 \div 25 \times \frac{6}{12}$			
~~Dec~~	~~31~~				
Dec	31	Rent Receivable		300	
		Rent Earned			300
Dec	31	Unearned Rent		670	
		Rent Earned .			670
Jan	~~1~~3	Salaries Expense .		405	
		Salaries Payable		270	
		Cash			675
~~Jan~~	~~12~~				
Jan	12	~~Rent Receivable~~		~~300~~	
Jan	12	Cash		600	
		Rent Receivable			300
		Rent Earned .			300

Part 2

DATE	ACCOUNT TITLES AND EXPLANATION	P.R.	DEBIT	CREDIT

GENERAL JOURNAL

DATE		ACCOUNT TITLES AND EXPLANATION	P.R.	DEBIT	CREDIT
Dec	31	Insurance Expense		7 7 5	
		Prepaid Insurance			7 7 5
Dec	31	Office Supplies Expense.		4 8 0	
		Office supplies			4 8 0
Dec	31	Depreciation Expense, Office Equipment		9 3 5	
		Accumulated Depreciation, Office Equipment			9 3 5
Dec	31	Depreciation Expense, Automobile		2 1 0 0	
		Accumulated Depreciation, Automobile			2 1 0 0
Dec	31	Unearned Management Fees.		3 6 0	
		Management Fees Earned.			3 6 0
Dec	31	Account Receivable		3 0 0	
		Management Fees Earned			3 0 0
Dec	31	Office salaries Expense		1 6 5	
		Office salaries Payable			1 6 5

GENERAL LEDGER

Cash   ACCT. NO. 111

DATE		EXPLANATION	P.R.	DEBIT	CREDIT	BALANCE
Dec	31			2 5 0 0		

Accounts Receivable   ACCT. NO. 112

DATE		EXPLANATION	P.R.	DEBIT	CREDIT	BALANCE
Dec	31			3 0 0		3 0 0

Prepaid Insurance   ACCT. NO. 113

DATE		EXPLANATION	P.R.	DEBIT	CREDIT	BALANCE
Dec	31			2 1 0 0		
					7 7 5	~~1 3 5 0~~
						1 3 2 5

Office Supplies   ACCT. NO. 114

DATE		EXPLANATION	P.R.	DEBIT	CREDIT	BALANCE
Dec	31			5 5 5		
Dec	31				4 8 0	7 5

Office Equipment   ACCT. NO. 131

DATE		EXPLANATION	P.R.	DEBIT	CREDIT	BALANCE
Dec	31			7 5 0 0		

Accumulated Depreciation, Office Equipment   ACCT. NO. 132

DATE	EXPLANATION	P.R.	DEBIT	CREDIT	BALANCE
Dec 31				2500	
Dec 31				935	3435

Automobile   ACCT. NO. 133

DATE	EXPLANATION	P.R.	DEBIT	CREDIT	BALANCE
Dec 31			15350		

Accumulated Depreciation, Automobile   ACCT. NO. 134

DATE	EXPLANATION	P.R.	DEBIT	CREDIT	BALANCE
Dec 31				3000	
Dec 31				2100	5100

Accounts Payable   ACCT. NO. 211

DATE	EXPLANATION	P.R.	DEBIT	CREDIT	BALANCE
Dec 31				275	

Office Salaries Payable   ACCT. NO. 212

DATE	EXPLANATION	P.R.	DEBIT	CREDIT	BALANCE
Dec 31				165	

Unearned Management Fees   ACCT. NO. 213

DATE	EXPLANATION	P.R.	DEBIT	CREDIT	BALANCE
Dec 31				540	
Dec 31			360		180

Don Miller, Capital   ACCT. NO. 311

DATE	EXPLANATION	P.R.	DEBIT	CREDIT	BALANCE
Rec 31				1 50 0 0	

Don Miller, Withdrawals   ACCT. NO. 312

DATE	EXPLANATION	P.R.	DEBIT	CREDIT	BALANCE
Dec 31			2 25 0 0		

Sales Commissions Earned   ACCT. NO. 411

DATE	EXPLANATION	P.R.	DEBIT	CREDIT	BALANCE
Dec 31				49 4 0 0	

Management Fees Earned   ACCT. NO. 412

DATE	EXPLANATION	P.R.	DEBIT	CREDIT	BALANCE
Rec 31				3 60	
Dec 31				3 0 0	6 60

Office Salaries Expense   ACCT. NO. 511

DATE	EXPLANATION	P.R.	DEBIT	CREDIT	BALANCE
Rec 31			1 2 3 60		1 25 2 5
			1 6 5		

Advertising Expense   ACCT. NO. 512

DATE	EXPLANATION	P.R.	DEBIT	CREDIT	BALANCE
Rec 31			1 2 0 0		

Rent Expense   ACCT. NO. 513

DATE	EXPLANATION	P.R.	DEBIT	CREDIT	BALANCE
Dec 31			6000		

Telephone Expense   ACCT. NO. 514

DATE	EXPLANATION	P.R.	DEBIT	CREDIT	BALANCE
Dec 31			650		

Insurance Expense   ACCT. NO. 515

DATE	EXPLANATION	P.R.	DEBIT	CREDIT	BALANCE
Dec 31			775		

Office Supplies Expense   ACCT. NO. 516

DATE	EXPLANATION	P.R.	DEBIT	CREDIT	BALANCE
Dec 51			480		
Dec 31			165		

Depreciation Expense, Office Equipment   ACCT. NO. 517

DATE	EXPLANATION	P.R.	DEBIT	CREDIT	BALANCE
Dec 31			835		

Depreciation Expense, Automobile   ACCT. NO. 518

DATE	EXPLANATION	P.R.	DEBIT	CREDIT	BALANCE
Dec 31			2100		

Century Realty
Adjust Trial Balance
Dec 31, 1993

	Debit	Credit
Cash	2500	
Account Receivble	300	
Prepaid Insurance	1325	
Office Supplies	75	
Office Equipment	7500	
Accumulated Repreciation, Office Equipment		3435
Automobile	15350	
Accumulated Depreciation, Automobile		5100
Account Payable		275
Office Salaries Payable		165
Unearned Management Fees		180
Don Miller, Capital		15000
Don Miller, Withdrew	22500	
Sales Commission Earned		49400
Management Fees Earned		660
Office Salaries Expense	12525	
Advertising Expense	1200	
Rent Expense	6000	
Telephone Expense	650	
Insurance Expense	775	
Office Supplies Expense	480	
Depreciation Expense, Office Equipment	835	
Depreciation Expense Automobile	2100	
	74240	74215
	74215	

Century Realty
Income Statement
For the ~~Dec~~ Month Ended. Dec 31, 1993

Revenue:

Sales Commission Earned.		4 9 4 0 0
Management Fees Earned		6 6 0.
Operating Expense:		
Office Salaries Expense.	1 2 5 2 5	
Advertising Expense	1 2 0 0	
Rent Expense.	6 0 0 0	
Telephone Expense	6 5 0	
Insurance Expense	7 7 5	
Office Supplies Expense	9 8 0	
Depreciation Expense. Office Equipment	9 3 5	
Depreciation Expense. , Automobile	2 1 0 0	
		2 4 6 6 5
Total Operating Expenses		
		2 5 3 9 5
Net income		

Century Realty
Statement of Change in Owner's Equity.
For the month Ended Dec 31, 1993.

Ron Miller, Capital, Nov 30, 93	$ 1 5 0 0 0		
Plus Net Income.	2 5 3 9 5	4 0 3 9 5	
Total		4 0 3 9 5	
Less: withdraw by owner		2 2 5 0 0	
Ron Mill, capital , Dec 31, 93		1 7 8 9 5	

47

GENERAL JOURNAL

DATE	ACCOUNT TITLES AND EXPLANATION	P.R.	DEBIT	CREDIT

GENERAL LEDGER

Cash   ACCT. NO. 111

DATE	EXPLANATION	P.R.	DEBIT	CREDIT	BALANCE

Accounts Receivable   ACCT. NO. 112

DATE	EXPLANATION	P.R.	DEBIT	CREDIT	BALANCE

Prepaid Insurance   ACCT. NO. 113

DATE	EXPLANATION	P.R.	DEBIT	CREDIT	BALANCE

Office Supplies   ACCT. NO. 114

DATE	EXPLANATION	P.R.	DEBIT	CREDIT	BALANCE

Investment in Trail, Inc., Common Stock   ACCT. NO. 121

DATE	EXPLANATION	P.R.	DEBIT	CREDIT	BALANCE

Office Equipment   ACCT. NO. 131

DATE	EXPLANATION	P.R.	DEBIT	CREDIT	BALANCE

Accumulated Depreciation, Office Equipment — ACCT. NO. 132

DATE		EXPLANATION	P.R.	DEBIT	CREDIT	BALANCE

Trucks — ACCT. NO. 133

DATE		EXPLANATION	P.R.	DEBIT	CREDIT	BALANCE

Accumulated Depreciation, Trucks — ACCT. NO. 134

DATE		EXPLANATION	P.R.	DEBIT	CREDIT	BALANCE

Building — ACCT. NO. 135

DATE		EXPLANATION	P.R.	DEBIT	CREDIT	BALANCE

Accumulated Depreciation, Building — ACCT. NO. 136

DATE		EXPLANATION	P.R.	DEBIT	CREDIT	BALANCE

Land — ACCT. NO. 137

DATE		EXPLANATION	P.R.	DEBIT	CREDIT	BALANCE

Franchise   ACCT. NO. 141

DATE	EXPLANATION	P.R.	DEBIT	CREDIT	BALANCE

Unearned Storage Fees   ACCT. NO. 212

DATE	EXPLANATION	P.R.	DEBIT	CREDIT	BALANCE

Salaries and Wages Payable   ACCT. NO. 213

DATE	EXPLANATION	P.R.	DEBIT	CREDIT	BALANCE

Long-Term Notes Payable   ACCT. NO. 231

DATE	EXPLANATION	P.R.	DEBIT	CREDIT	BALANCE

Dennis Meade, Capital   ACCT. NO. 311

DATE	EXPLANATION	P.R.	DEBIT	CREDIT	BALANCE

Dennis Meade, Withdrawals   ACCT. NO. 312

DATE	EXPLANATION	P.R.	DEBIT	CREDIT	BALANCE

Revenue from Moving Services   ACCT. NO. 411

DATE	EXPLANATION	P.R.	DEBIT	CREDIT	BALANCE

Storage Fees Earned   ACCT. NO. 412

DATE	EXPLANATION	P.R.	DEBIT	CREDIT	BALANCE

Office Salaries Expense   ACCT. NO. 511

DATE	EXPLANATION	P.R.	DEBIT	CREDIT	BALANCE

Drivers' and Helpers' Wages Expense   ACCT. NO. 512

DATE	EXPLANATION	P.R.	DEBIT	CREDIT	BALANCE

Gas, Oil, and Repairs Expense   ACCT. NO. 513

DATE	EXPLANATION	P.R.	DEBIT	CREDIT	BALANCE

Insurance Expense   ACCT. NO. 514

DATE	EXPLANATION	P.R.	DEBIT	CREDIT	BALANCE

Office Supplies Expense   ACCT. NO. 515

DATE		EXPLANATION	P.R.	DEBIT	CREDIT	BALANCE

Depreciation Expense, Office Equipment   ACCT. NO. 516

DATE		EXPLANATION	P.R.	DEBIT	CREDIT	BALANCE

Depreciation Expense, Trucks   ACCT. NO. 517

DATE		EXPLANATION	P.R.	DEBIT	CREDIT	BALANCE

Depreciation Expense, Building   ACCT. NO. 518

DATE		EXPLANATION	P.R.	DEBIT	CREDIT	BALANCE

Interest Expense   ACCT. NO. 519

DATE		EXPLANATION	P.R.	DEBIT	CREDIT	BALANCE

GENERAL JOURNAL

DATE	ACCOUNT TITLES AND EXPLANATION	P.R.	DEBIT	CREDIT

GENERAL LEDGER

Cash   **ACCT. NO. 111**

DATE	EXPLANATION	P.R.	DEBIT	CREDIT	BALANCE

Accounts Receivable   **ACCT. NO. 112**

DATE	EXPLANATION	P.R.	DEBIT	CREDIT	BALANCE

Prepaid Insurance   **ACCT. NO. 113**

DATE	EXPLANATION	P.R.	DEBIT	CREDIT	BALANCE

Office Supplies   **ACCT. NO. 114**

DATE	EXPLANATION	P.R.	DEBIT	CREDIT	BALANCE

Office Equipment   **ACCT. NO. 131**

DATE	EXPLANATION	P.R.	DEBIT	CREDIT	BALANCE

Accumulated Depreciation, Office Equipment   **ACCT. NO. 132**

DATE	EXPLANATION	P.R.	DEBIT	CREDIT	BALANCE

Buildings and Improvements   ACCT. NO. 133

DATE		EXPLANATION	P.R.	DEBIT	CREDIT	BALANCE

Accumulated Depreciation, Buildings and Improvements   ACCT. NO. 134

DATE		EXPLANATION	P.R.	DEBIT	CREDIT	BALANCE

Land   ACCT. NO. 135

DATE		EXPLANATION	P.R.	DEBIT	CREDIT	BALANCE

Wages Payable   ACCT. NO. 212

DATE		EXPLANATION	P.R.	DEBIT	CREDIT	BALANCE

Property Taxes Payable   ACCT. NO. 213

DATE		EXPLANATION	P.R.	DEBIT	CREDIT	BALANCE

Interest Payable   ACCT. NO. 214

DATE		EXPLANATION	P.R.	DEBIT	CREDIT	BALANCE

Unearned Rent   ACCT. NO. 215

DATE	EXPLANATION	P.R.	DEBIT	CREDIT	BALANCE

Long-Term Notes Payable   ACCT. NO. 231

DATE	EXPLANATION	P.R.	DEBIT	CREDIT	BALANCE

Ida Henry, Capital   ACCT. NO. 311

DATE	EXPLANATION	P.R.	DEBIT	CREDIT	BALANCE

Ida Henry, Withdrawals   ACCT. NO. 312

DATE	EXPLANATION	P.R.	DEBIT	CREDIT	BALANCE

Rent Earned   ACCT. NO. 411

DATE	EXPLANATION	P.R.	DEBIT	CREDIT	BALANCE

Wages Expense   ACCT. NO. 511

DATE	EXPLANATION	P.R.	DEBIT	CREDIT	BALANCE

Utilities Expense — ACCT. NO. 512

DATE	EXPLANATION	P.R.	DEBIT	CREDIT	BALANCE

Property Taxes Expense — ACCT. NO. 513

DATE	EXPLANATION	P.R.	DEBIT	CREDIT	BALANCE

Insurance Expense — ACCT. NO. 514

DATE	EXPLANATION	P.R.	DEBIT	CREDIT	BALANCE

Office Supplies Expense — ACCT. NO. 515

DATE	EXPLANATION	P.R.	DEBIT	CREDIT	BALANCE

Depreciation Expense, Office Equipment — ACCT. NO. 516

DATE	EXPLANATION	P.R.	DEBIT	CREDIT	BALANCE

Depreciation Expense, Buildings and Improvements — ACCT. NO. 517

DATE	EXPLANATION	P.R.	DEBIT	CREDIT	BALANCE

Interest Expense   ACCT. NO. 518

DATE		EXPLANATION	P.R.	DEBIT	CREDIT	BALANCE

GENERAL JOURNAL

DATE	ACCOUNT TITLES AND EXPLANATION	P.R.	DEBIT	CREDIT

Part 1   **GENERAL JOURNAL**

DATE	ACCOUNT TITLES AND EXPLANATION	P.R.	DEBIT	CREDIT

Part 2

GENERAL JOURNAL

DATE		ACCOUNT TITLES AND EXPLANATION	P.R.	DEBIT	CREDIT

(The work sheet for this problem is in the back of this booklet.)

Rip's Repair Services

Income Statement

For the Month Ended December 31, 1990.

Revenue :		
Revenue From Repair		$55845
Operating expense :		
Wages Expense	$15330	
Rent Expense	4500	
Utilities Expense	975	
Insurance Expense	800	
Repair Supplies Expense :	3215	
Depreciation Expense, Repair Equipment	990	
Total Operating Expense		25810
Net Income		$30035
R		

Rip's Repair Services

Statement of Changes in Owner's Equity

For the month Ended December 31, 1990

Rip Horn, capital Nov 30, 1990		06185
Plus:	30035	
Net Income	30035	30035
Total		36220
Less withdraw by Owner.		28200
Rip Horn, Capital Dec 31, 1990		8020

Rip's Repair Services
Balance Sheet
Dec 31, 1990

Assets

Current assets:			
Cash		$ 1825	
Prepaid Insurance		500	
Repair Supplies		1160	
Total Current assets			$ 3485
Plant and Equipment:			
Repair Equipment	$ 7860		
Less accumulated depreciation	2910	4950	
Total plant and equipment			4950
Total Assets :			$ 8435

Liabilities

Current liabilities			
Accounts payable	295		
Wages payable	120		
Total current Liabilities		415	
Total Liabilities :			415

Owner's Equity

Rip Horn, capital			
			8020
Total liabilities and owner's equity			$ 8435

GENERAL JOURNAL

DATE		ACCOUNT TITLES AND EXPLANATION	P.R.	DEBIT	CREDIT
Dec	31	Insurance Expense		8 00	
		Prepaid Insurance			8 00
Dec	31	Wages Expense		1 20	
		Wages Payable			1 20
Dec	31	Repair Supplies Expense		3 2 15	
		Repair Supplies			3 2 15
Dec	31	Depreciation Expense, Repair Equipment		9 00	
		Accumulated Depreciation, Repair Equipment			9 00
		Closing Entries			
Dec	31	Revenue From Repair		55 8 45	
		Income Summary			55 8 45
Dec	31	Income Summary		25 8 10	
		Wages Expense			15 3 30
		Rent Expense			45 00
		Utilities Expense			9 75
		Insurance Expense			8 00
		Repair Supplies Expense			3 2 15
		Depreciation Expense			9 90
Dec	31	Income Summary		30 0 35	
		Rip Hans, Capital			30 0 35
Dec	31	Rip Hans, Capital		28 2 00	
		Rip Hans, Withdrawals.			28 2 00

DATE	ACCOUNT TITLES AND EXPLANATION	P.R.	DEBIT	CREDIT

GENERAL JOURNAL   PAGE 1

DATE		ACCOUNT TITLES AND EXPLANATION	P.R.	DEBIT	CREDIT
May	2	Cash		3500	
		Automobile		12000	
		Tami, Martin, Capital			15500
May	2	Rent Expense		600	
		Cash			600
May	2	Prepaid Insurance		996	
		Cash			996
May	3				
May	3	Office Supplies		210	
		Cash			210
May	13	Salaries Expense		670	
		Cash			670
May	19	Cash		2400	
		Commissions Earned			2400
May	27	Salaries Expense		670	
		Cash			670
May	31	Telephone Expense		65	
		Cash			65
May	31	Gas Oil and Repair Expense		70	
		Cash			70
May	31	Insurance expense		83	
		Prepaid Insurance			83
May	31	Office Supplies Expense		45	
		Office Supplies			45
May	31	Depreciation Expense, Auto		240	
		Accumulated Depreciation, Auto			240
May	31	Salaries Expense		134	
		Salaries Payable			134

DATE		ACCOUNT TITLES AND EXPLANATION	P.R.	DEBIT	CREDIT
May Dec	31	Commss Commission Earned		2400	
		Income Summary			2400
May	31	Income Summary		2577	
		Rent Expense			600
		Salaries Expense			1474
		Gas Oil Repair Expense			70
		Telephone Expense			65
		Insurance Expense			83
		Depreciation Expense			240
		Office Supply Expense			45
May	31	Tami Martin Capital		177	
		Income Summary			177
June					
Jan	1	Rent Expense		600	
		Cash			600
6	5	Cash		7275	
		Commission Earned			7275
6	7	Tami Martin, Withdrawals		2250	
		Cash			2250
6	10	Salaries Expense		670	
		Cash			670
6	21	Office supplies		55	
		Cash			55
6	24	Salaries Expense		670	
		Cash			670
6	30	Telephone Expense		60	
		Cash			60
6	30	Gas Oil Repair Expense		75	
		Cash			75

DATE		ACCOUNT TITLES AND EXPLANATION	P.R.	DEBIT	CREDIT
6	30	Insurance Expense		83	
		Prepaid Insurance			83
6	30	Office Supplies Expense		40	
		Office Supply			40
6	30	Depreciation Exp.		240	
		Accumulated Depreciation, Auto.			240
6	30	Salaries Exp.		268	
		Salaries Payable			268
6	30	Commission Earned		7275	
		Income Summary			7275
6	30	Income Summary		2706	
		Rent Exp.			600
		Salaries Exp.			1608
		Gas Oil Repair Exp.			75
		Telephone Exp.			60
		Insurance Exp.			83
		Depreciation Exp. Auto.			240
		Office Supply Expense			40
6	30	Income Summary		4569	
		T. M. Capital			4569
6	30	TM Capital		2250	
		TM Withdrawals			2250

DATE	ACCOUNT TITLES AND EXPLANATION	P.R.	DEBIT	CREDIT

GENERAL LEDGER

Cash   ACCT. NO. 111

DATE	EXPLANATION	P.R.	DEBIT	CREDIT	BALANCE
May 2			3500		
May 2				600	2900
May 2				996	1904
May 3				210	1694
May 13				670	1024
May 19			2400		3424
May 27				670	2754
May 31				65	2689
May 31				70	2619
6 1				600	2019
6 5			7275		9294
6 7				2250	7044
6 7				670	6374
6 21				55	6319
6 24				670	5649
6 30				60	5589
6 30				75	5514

Prepaid Insurance   ACCT. NO. 113

DATE	EXPLANATION	P.R.	DEBIT	CREDIT	BALANCE
May 2			996		
May 31				83	913
6 30				83	830

Office Supplies   ACCT. NO. 114

DATE	EXPLANATION	P.R.	DEBIT	CREDIT	BALANCE
May 3			210		
May 31				45	165
6 21			55		220
6 30			40		180

Automobile   ACCT. NO. 13

DATE		EXPLANATION	P.R.	DEBIT	CREDIT	BALANCE
May	2			1200 0		120 0 0

Accumulated Depreciation, Automobile   ACCT. NO. 13

DATE		EXPLANATION	P.R.	DEBIT	CREDIT	BALANCE
May	31				240	240
6	30				240	480

Salaries Payable   ACCT. NO. 21

DATE		EXPLANATION	P.R.	DEBIT	CREDIT	BALANCE
May	31				134	134
6	30				268	402

Tami Martin, Capital   ACCT. NO. 31

DATE		EXPLANATION	P.R.	DEBIT	CREDIT	BALANCE
May	2				15500	15500
May	31			177		15323
6	30				4569	19892
6	30			2250		17642

Tami Martin, Withdrawals   ACCT. NO. 312

DATE		EXPLANATION	P.R.	DEBIT	CREDIT	BALANCE
6	7			2250		2250
6	30				2250	-0-

Income Summary   ACCT. NO. 313

DATE		EXPLANATION	P.R.	DEBIT	CREDIT	BALANCE
May 31					2400	2400
May 31				2577		(177)
May 31					177	-0-
6	30				7275	7275
6	30			2706		4569
6	30			4569		-0-

Commissions Earned   ACCT. NO. 411

DATE	EXPLANATION	P.R.	DEBIT	CREDIT	BALANCE
May 19				2400	2400
May 31			2400		— 0 —
6 5				7275	7275
6 30			7275		— 0 —

Rent Expense   ACCT. NO. 511

DATE	EXPLANATION	P.R.	DEBIT	CREDIT	BALANCE
May 2			600		
May 31				600	— 0 —
6 1			600		600
6 30				600	— 0 —

Salaries Expense   ACCT. NO. 512

DATE	EXPLANATION	P.R.	DEBIT	CREDIT	BALANCE
May 13			670		670
May 27			670		1340
May 31			134		1474
May 31				1474	— 0 —
6 10			670		670
6 24			670		1340
6 30			268		1608
6 30			1608	1608	— 0 —

Gas, Oil, and Repairs Expense   ACCT. NO. 513

DATE	EXPLANATION	P.R.	DEBIT	CREDIT	BALANCE
May 31			70		70
May 31				70	— 0 —
6 30			75		75
6 30				75	— 0 —

Telephone Expense   ACCT. NO. 514

DATE	EXPLANATION	P.R.	DEBIT	CREDIT	BALANCE
May 27			65		65
May 31				65	—0—
6 30			60		60
6 30				60	—0—

Insurance Expense   ACCT. NO. 515

DATE	EXPLANATION	P.R.	DEBIT	CREDIT	BALANCE
May 31			83		83
May 31				83	—0—
6 30			83		83
6 30				83	—0—

Office Supplies Expense   ACCT. NO. 516

DATE	EXPLANATION	P.R.	DEBIT	CREDIT	BALANCE
May 31			45		45
May 31				45	—0—
6 30			40		40
6 30				40	—0—

Depreciation Expense, Automobile   ACCT. NO. 517

DATE	EXPLANATION	P.R.	DEBIT	CREDIT	BALANCE
May 31			240		240
May 31				240	—0—
6 30			240		240
6 30				240	—0—

MARTIN REALTY
Work Sheet
For Month Ended May 31, 1990

ACCOUNT TITLES	UNADJUSTED TRIAL BALANCE DR.	CR.	ADJUSTMENTS DR.	CR.	ADJUSTED TRIAL BALANCE DR.	CR.	INCOME STATEMENT DR.	CR.	STATEMENT OF CHANGES IN OWNER'S EQUITY OR BALANCE SHEET DR.	CR.
Cash	2618				2618				2618	
Prepaid Insurance	996			(a) 83	913				913	
Office Supplies	210			(b) 45	165				165	
Automobile	12000				12000				12000	
Salaries Payable				(d) 134		134				134
Tami Martin, Capital		15500				15500				15500
Tami Martin, Withdrawals										
Commission Earned		2400				2400		2400		
Rent Expense	600				600		600			
Salaries Expense	1340		(d) 134		1474		1474			
Gas, Oil and Repair Expense	70				70		70			
Telephone Expense	65				65		65			
	17900	17900								
Insurance Expense			(a) 83		83		83			
Office Supplies Expense			(b) 45		45		45			
Depreciation Expense, Auto			(c) 240		240		240			
Accumulated Dep., Auto				(c) 240		240				240
			502	502	18274	18274	2577	2400	15697	15874
Net Income (Loss)								(177)	177	
							2577	2577	15874	15874

MARTIN REALTY
Work Sheet
For Month Ended June 30, 1990

ACCOUNT TITLES	UNADJUSTED TRIAL BALANCE DR.	CR.	ADJUSTMENTS DR.	CR.	ADJUSTED TRIAL BALANCE DR.	CR.	INCOME STATEMENT DR.	CR.	STATEMENT OF CHANGES IN OWNER'S EQUITY OR BALANCE SHEET DR.	CR.
Cash	5514				5514				5514	
Prepaid Insurance	913			(a)83	830				830	
Office Supply	220			(b)40	180				180	
Auto	12000				12000				12000	
Accumulate Dep. Auto		240		(c)240		480				480
Salaries Payable		134		(d)268		402				402
T.M., Capital		15323				15323				15323
T.M., Withdrawals	2250				2250				2250	
Commission Earned		7275				7275		7275		
Rent Expense	600				600		600			
Salaries Expense	1340		(d)268		1608		1608			
Gas & Gen R. Expense	75				75		75			
Tel Expense	60				60		60			
	20772	22972								
Insurance Expense			(a)83		83		83			
Office Supplies Exp.			(b)40		40		40			
Depreciation Exp. Auto			(c)240		240		240			
			631	631	23480	23480	2706	7275	20774	16205
Net Income							4569			4569
							7275	7275	20774	20774

MARTIN REALTY

Income Statement

For Month Ended May 31, 1990

Revenue:		
Commission Earned.		2400
Operating Expense:		
Rent Expense	600	
Salaries Expense	1474	
Gas Oil and Repair Expense	70	
Telephone Expense	65	
Insurance Expense	83	
Office Supplies Expense	45	
Depreciation Expense	240	
Total Operating Expenses.		2577
Net Income		(177)

MARTIN REALTY

Statement of Changes in Owner's Equity

For Month Ended May 31, 1990

Tami Martin, capital April 30, 1990		-0-
plus:		
Investments by owner.	15500	
Net Income	(177)	
Total		15323
Less: Withdrawals by Owner		0
Tami Martin, capital May 31, 1990		15323

MARTIN REALTY

Balance Sheet

May 31, 1990

Assets						
Current Assets :						
Cash			$ 2619			
Prepaid Insurance			913			
Office supplies			165			
Total current Assets					$ 3697	
plant and equipment .						
Automobile	12000					
Less Accumulated Depreciation, Auto	240		11760		11760	
Total Assets					15475	
Liabilities						
Current Liabilities						
Salaries payable	134		63			
Total Liabilities			134		134	
Owner's Equity					15323	
Tami. Marti , Capital					15323	
Total Owners & Liabilities and Owners Equity					15457	

MARTIN REALTY

Post-Closing Trial Balance

May 31, 1990

Cash	2619	
Prepaid Insurance	913	
Office Supplies	165	
Automobile	12000	
Accumulated Depreciation, Auto		240
Salaries Payable		134
Tami Martin , Capital		15323
	15697	15697

MARTIN REALTY

Income Statement

For Month Ended June 30, 1990

Revenue :					
Commission Earned .					$7275
Operating Expense :					
Rent Expense	$	600			
Salaries Expense		1608			
Gas Oil and Repair Expense .		75			
Tel Expense		60			
Insurance Exp .		83			
Office Supply Exp .		40			
Dep . Exp . Auto .		240			2706
Total Operating Expense .					2706
Net Income					$4569

MARTIN REALTY

Statement of Changes in Owner's Equity

For Month Ended June 30, 1990

Tami Martin , Capital May 31					15323
Plus :					
Net Income .		4569			4569
Total					19892
Less : withdrawls by owner .					2250
Tami Martin , Capital June 30, 1980					17642

MARTIN REALTY

Balance Sheet

June 30, 1990

Assets			
Current Assets :			
Cash		5514	
Prepaid Insurance		830	
Office Supplies		180	
Total Current Assets			6524
Plant and Equipment ·			
Auto ·	12000		
Less : Accumulated Depreciation , Auto	480	11520	11520
Total Assets :			18044
Liabilities			
Current Liabilities :			
Salaries Payable	402		
Total Liabilities		402	402
Owner's Eq ·			t 7642
T M Capital			17642
			18044
Total Liabilities and Owner's Eq.			

MARTIN REALTY

Post-Closing Trial Balance

June 30, 1990

Cash	5514	
Prepaid Insurance	830	
Office Supplies	180	
Auto ·	12000	
Accumulated Depreciation Auto		480
Salaries Payable		402
T M Capital		17642
	18524	18524

(The work sheet for this problem is in the back of this booklet.)

GENERAL JOURNAL   PAGE 1

DATE	ACCOUNT TITLES AND EXPLANATION	P.R.	DEBIT	CREDIT

DATE		ACCOUNT TITLES AND EXPLANATION	P.R.	DEBIT	CREDIT

Cash   ACCT. NO. 111

DATE		EXPLANATION	P.R.	DEBIT	CREDIT	BALANCE

Bowling Supplies   ACCT. NO. 112

DATE		EXPLANATION	P.R.	DEBIT	CREDIT	BALANCE

Prepaid Insurance   ACCT. NO. 113

DATE		EXPLANATION	P.R.	DEBIT	CREDIT	BALANCE

Prepaid Interest   ACCT. NO. 114

DATE		EXPLANATION	P.R.	DEBIT	CREDIT	BALANCE

Bowling Equipment   ACCT. NO. 131

DATE		EXPLANATION	P.R.	DEBIT	CREDIT	BALANCE

Accumulated Depreciation, Bowling Equipment   ACCT. NO. 132

DATE	EXPLANATION	P.R.	DEBIT	CREDIT	BALANCE

Accounts Payable   ACCT. NO. 211

DATE	EXPLANATION	P.R.	DEBIT	CREDIT	BALANCE

Wages Payable   ACCT. NO. 212

DATE	EXPLANATION	P.R.	DEBIT	CREDIT	BALANCE

Rent Payable   ACCT. NO. 213

DATE	EXPLANATION	P.R.	DEBIT	CREDIT	BALANCE

Taxes Payable   ACCT. NO. 214

DATE	EXPLANATION	P.R.	DEBIT	CREDIT	BALANCE

Long-Term Notes Payable   ACCT. NO. 231

DATE	EXPLANATION	P.R.	DEBIT	CREDIT	BALANCE

Paul Strait, Capital   ACCT. NO. 311

DATE	EXPLANATION	P.R.	DEBIT	CREDIT	BALANCE

Paul Strait, Withdrawals   ACCT. NO. 312

DATE	EXPLANATION	P.R.	DEBIT	CREDIT	BALANCE

Income Summary   ACCT. NO. 313

DATE	EXPLANATION	P.R.	DEBIT	CREDIT	BALANCE

Bowling Revenue   ACCT. NO. 411

DATE	EXPLANATION	P.R.	DEBIT	CREDIT	BALANCE

Wages Expense   ACCT. NO. 511

DATE		EXPLANATION	P.R.	DEBIT	CREDIT	BALANCE

Equipment Repairs Expense   ACCT. NO. 512

DATE		EXPLANATION	P.R.	DEBIT	CREDIT	BALANCE

Rent Expense   ACCT. NO. 513

DATE		EXPLANATION	P.R.	DEBIT	CREDIT	BALANCE

Utilities Expense   ACCT. NO. 514

DATE		EXPLANATION	P.R.	DEBIT	CREDIT	BALANCE

Taxes Expense   ACCT. NO. 515

DATE		EXPLANATION	P.R.	DEBIT	CREDIT	BALANCE

Bowling Supplies Expense   ACCT. NO. 516

DATE		EXPLANATION	P.R.	DEBIT	CREDIT	BALANCE

Insurance Expense   ACCT. NO. 517

DATE		EXPLANATION	P.R.	DEBIT	CREDIT	BALANCE

Depreciation Expense, Bowling Equipment   ACCT. NO. 518

DATE		EXPLANATION	P.R.	DEBIT	CREDIT	BALANCE

Interest Expense   ACCT. NO. 519

DATE		EXPLANATION	P.R.	DEBIT	CREDIT	BALANCE

STRAIT ALLEYS

Income Statement

For Year Ended December 31, 1990

STRAIT ALLEYS

Statement of Changes in Owner's Equity

For Year Ended December 31, 1990

STRAIT ALLEYS

Balance Sheet

December 31, 1990

STRAIT ALLEYS

Post-Closing Trial Balance

December 31, 1990

DOC'S DELIVERY SERVICE

Income Statement

For Year Ended December 31, 1990

DOC'S DELIVERY SERVICE

Statement of Changes in Owner's Equity

For Year Ended December 31, 1990

DOC'S DELIVERY SERVICE

Balance Sheet

December 31, 1990

GENERAL JOURNAL

DATE	ACCOUNT TITLES AND EXPLANATION	P.R.	DEBIT	CREDIT

DATE	ACCOUNT TITLES AND EXPLANATION	P.R.	DEBIT	CREDIT

Cash   ACCT. NO. 111

DATE	EXPLANATION	P.R.	DEBIT	CREDIT	BALANCE

Accounts Receivable   ACCT. NO. 112

DATE	EXPLANATION	P.R.	DEBIT	CREDIT	BALANCE

Prepaid Insurance   ACCT. NO. 113

DATE	EXPLANATION	P.R.	DEBIT	CREDIT	BALANCE

Office Supplies   ACCT. NO. 114

DATE	EXPLANATION	P.R.	DEBIT	CREDIT	BALANCE

Prepaid Rent   ACCT. NO. 115

DATE	EXPLANATION	P.R.	DEBIT	CREDIT	BALANCE

Office Equipment   ACCT. NO.   131

DATE		EXPLANATION	P.R.	DEBIT	CREDIT	BALANCE

Accumulated Depreciation, Office Equipment   ACCT. NO.   132

DATE		EXPLANATION	P.R.	DEBIT	CREDIT	BALANCE

Delivery Equipment   ACCT. NO.   133

DATE		EXPLANATION	P.R.	DEBIT	CREDIT	BALANCE

Accumulated Depreciation, Delivery Equipment   ACCT. NO.   134

DATE		EXPLANATION	P.R.	DEBIT	CREDIT	BALANCE

Accounts Payable   ACCT. NO.   211

DATE		EXPLANATION	P.R.	DEBIT	CREDIT	BALANCE

Rent Payable   ACCT. NO. 212

DATE	EXPLANATION	P.R.	DEBIT	CREDIT	BALANCE

Salaries and Wages Payable   ACCT. NO. 213

DATE	EXPLANATION	P.R.	DEBIT	CREDIT	BALANCE

Unearned Delivery Service Revenue   ACCT. NO. 214

DATE	EXPLANATION	P.R.	DEBIT	CREDIT	BALANCE

Mark Welby, Capital   ACCT. NO. 311

DATE	EXPLANATION	P.R.	DEBIT	CREDIT	BALANCE

Mark Welby, Withdrawals   ACCT. NO. 312

DATE	EXPLANATION	P.R.	DEBIT	CREDIT	BALANCE

Income Summary   ACCT. NO.   313

DATE		EXPLANATION	P.R.	DEBIT	CREDIT	BALANCE

Delivery Service Revenue   ACCT. NO.   411

DATE		EXPLANATION	P.R.	DEBIT	CREDIT	BALANCE

Rent Expense   ACCT. NO.   511

DATE		EXPLANATION	P.R.	DEBIT	CREDIT	BALANCE

Telephone Expense   ACCT. NO.   512

DATE		EXPLANATION	P.R.	DEBIT	CREDIT	BALANCE

Office Salaries Expense   ACCT. NO.   513

DATE		EXPLANATION	P.R.	DEBIT	CREDIT	BALANCE

Insurance Expense, Office Equipment   ACCT. NO. 514

DATE	EXPLANATION	P.R.	DEBIT	CREDIT	BALANCE

Office Supplies Expense   ACCT. NO. 515

DATE	EXPLANATION	P.R.	DEBIT	CREDIT	BALANCE

Depreciation Expense, Office Equipment   ACCT. NO. 516

DATE	EXPLANATION	P.R.	DEBIT	CREDIT	BALANCE

Delivery Wages Expense   ACCT. NO. 517

DATE	EXPLANATION	P.R.	DEBIT	CREDIT	BALANCE

Gas, Oil, and Repairs Expense   ACCT. NO. 518

DATE	EXPLANATION	P.R.	DEBIT	CREDIT	BALANCE

Insurance Expense, Delivery Equipment   ACCT. NO.   519

DATE		EXPLANATION	P.R.	DEBIT	CREDIT	BALANCE

Depreciation Expense, Delivery Equipment   ACCT. NO.   520

DATE		EXPLANATION	P.R.	DEBIT	CREDIT	BALANCE

DOC'S DELIVERY SERVICE

Post-Closing Trial Balance

December 31, 1990

GENERAL JOURNAL

DATE	ACCOUNT TITLES AND EXPLANATION	P.R.	DEBIT	CREDIT

DATE		ACCOUNT TITLES AND EXPLANATION	P.R.	DEBIT	CREDIT

COMPREHENSIVE PROBLEM, Satellite Theatre   Name _____

GENERAL JOURNAL   PAGE 1

DATE	ACCOUNT TITLES AND EXPLANATION	P.R.	DEBIT	CREDIT

113

DATE	ACCOUNT TITLES AND EXPLANATION	P.R.	DEBIT	CREDIT

COMPREHENSIVE PROBLEM, Satellite Theatre (Continued)   Name _____

PAGE 3

DATE	ACCOUNT TITLES AND EXPLANATION	P.R.	DEBIT	CREDIT

GENERAL LEDGER

Cash   ACCT. NO. 11

DATE		EXPLANATION	P.R.	DEBIT	CREDIT	BALANCE
Nov.	30	Balance	√			4 0 0 0 00

Concessions Inventory   ACCT. NO. 112

DATE		EXPLANATION	P.R.	DEBIT	CREDIT	BALANCE
Nov.	30	Balance	√			11 2 0 0 00

Supplies Inventory   ACCT. NO. 11

DATE		EXPLANATION	P.R.	DEBIT	CREDIT	BALANCE
Nov.	30	Balance	√			7 5 0 00

Prepaid Movie Rental   ACCT. NO. 11

DATE		EXPLANATION	P.R.	DEBIT	CREDIT	BALANCE
Nov.	30	Balance	√			8 8 0 00

116

Equipment   ACCT. NO. 131

DATE		EXPLANATION	P.R.	DEBIT	CREDIT	BALANCE
Nov.	30	Balance	√			5 5 0 0 00

Accumulated Depreciation Equipment   ACCT. NO. 132

DATE		EXPLANATION	P.R.	DEBIT	CREDIT	BALANCE
Nov.	30	Balance	√			1 1 0 0 00

Building   ACCT. NO. 135

DATE		EXPLANATION	P.R.	DEBIT	CREDIT	BALANCE
Nov.	30	Balance	√			75 0 0 0 00

Accumulated Depreciation, Building   ACCT. NO. 136

DATE		EXPLANATION	P.R.	DEBIT	CREDIT	BALANCE
Nov.	30	Balance	√			14 5 0 0 00

Accounts Payable   ACCT. NO. 211

DATE		EXPLANATION	P.R.	DEBIT	CREDIT	BALANCE
Nov.	30	Balance	√			1 5 5 0 00

Wages Payable   ACCT. NO. 212

DATE		EXPLANATION	P.R.	DEBIT	CREDIT	BALANCE

Utilities Payable

ACCT. NO. 213

DATE		EXPLANATION	P.R.	DEBIT	CREDIT	BALANCE
Nov.	30	Balance	√			2 5 0 00

Interest Payable

ACCT. NO. 214

DATE		EXPLANATION	P.R.	DEBIT	CREDIT	BALANCE

Long-Term Notes Payable

ACCT. NO. 231

DATE		EXPLANATION	P.R.	DEBIT	CREDIT	BALANCE
Nov.	30	Balance	√			42 0 0 0 00

J.R. Thompson, Capital

ACCT. NO. 311

DATE		EXPLANATION	P.R.	DEBIT	CREDIT	BALANCE
Nov.	30	Balance	√			14 9 7 0 00

J.R. Thompson, Withdrawals

ACCT. NO. 312

DATE		EXPLANATION	P.R.	DEBIT	CREDIT	BALANCE
Nov.	30	Balance	√			8 0 0 0 00

Income Summary — ACCT. NO. 313

DATE		EXPLANATION	P.R.	DEBIT	CREDIT	BALANCE

Admissions Revenue — ACCT. NO. 411

DATE		EXPLANATION	P.R.	DEBIT	CREDIT	BALANCE
Nov.	30	Balance	√			39 850 00

Concessions Revenue — ACCT. NO. 412

DATE		EXPLANATION	P.R.	DEBIT	CREDIT	BALANCE
Nov.	30	Balance	√			28 650 00

Wages Expense — ACCT. NO. 511

DATE		EXPLANATION	P.R.	DEBIT	CREDIT	BALANCE
Nov.	30	Balance	√			14 000 00

Movie Rental Expense   ACCT. NO. 51

DATE		EXPLANATION	P.R.	DEBIT	CREDIT	BALANCE
Nov.	30	Balance	√			16 5 0 0 00

Concessions Expense   ACCT. NO. 51

DATE		EXPLANATION	P.R.	DEBIT	CREDIT	BALANCE

Supplies Expense   ACCT. NO. 51

DATE		EXPLANATION	P.R.	DEBIT	CREDIT	BALANCE

Utilties Expense   ACCT. NO. 51

DATE		EXPLANATION	P.R.	DEBIT	CREDIT	BALANCE
Nov.	30	Balance	√			2 8 0 0 00

Advertising Expense   ACCT. NO. 51

DATE		EXPLANATION	P.R.	DEBIT	CREDIT	BALANCE
Nov.	30	Balance	√			3 2 0 0 00

Maintenance Expense   ACCT. NO. 517

DATE		EXPLANATION	P.R.	DEBIT	CREDIT	BALANCE
Nov.	30	Balance	√			1 0 4 0 00

Depreciation Expense, Equipment   ACCT. NO. 518

DATE		EXPLANATION	P.R.	DEBIT	CREDIT	BALANCE

Depreciation Expense, Building   ACCT. NO. 519

DATE		EXPLANATION	P.R.	DEBIT	CREDIT	BALANCE

Interest Expense   ACCT. NO. 520

DATE		EXPLANATION	P.R.	DEBIT	CREDIT	BALANCE

SATELLITE THEATRE

Work Sheet for Year Ended December 31, 1990

ACCOUNT TITLES	UNADJUSTED TRIAL BALANCE		ADJUSTMENTS		ADJUSTED TRIAL BALANCE		INCOME STATEMENT		STATEMENT OF CHANGES IN OWNER'S EQUITY OR BALANCE SHEET	
	DR.	CR.	DR.	CR.	DR.	CR.	DR.	CR.	DR.	CR.
Cash										
Concessions inventory										
Supplies inventory										
Prepaid movie rental										
Equipment										
Accum. depr., equipment										
Building										
Accum. depr., building										
Accounts payable										
Wages payable										
Utilities payable										
Interest payable										
Long-term notes payable										
J.R. Thompson, capital										
J.R. Thompson, withdrawals										
Admissions revenue										
Concessions revenue										
Wages expense										
Movie rental expense										
Concessions expense										
Supplies expense										
Utilities expense										
Advertising expense										
Maintenance expense										
Depr. expense, equipment										
Depr. expense, building										
Interest expense										
Net income										

126

PAGE 1

DATE	ACCOUNT TITLES AND EXPLANATION	P.R.	DEBIT	CREDIT

GENERAL JOURNAL

DATE	ACCOUNT TITLES AND EXPLANATION	P.R.	DEBIT	CREDIT

GENERAL JOURNAL

DATE		ACCOUNT TITLES AND EXPLANATION	P.R.	DEBIT	CREDIT

DATE	ACCOUNT TITLES AND EXPLANATION	P.R.	DEBIT	CREDIT

Merchandise Inventory

DATE	EXPLANATION	P.R.	DEBIT	CREDIT	BALANCE

(The work sheet for this problem is in the back of this booklet.)

GENERAL JOURNAL

DATE	ACCOUNT TITLES AND EXPLANATION	P.R.	DEBIT	CREDIT

DATE	ACCOUNT TITLES AND EXPLANATION	P.R.	DEBIT	CREDIT

Merchandise Inventory

DATE	EXPLANATION	P.R.	DEBIT	CREDIT	BALANCE

(The work sheet for this problem is in the back of this booklet.)

GENERAL JOURNAL

DATE		ACCOUNT TITLES AND EXPLANATION	P.R.	DEBIT	CREDIT

DATE	ACCOUNT TITLES AND EXPLANATION	P.R.	DEBIT	CREDIT

Merchandise Inventory

DATE	EXPLANATION	P.R.	DEBIT	CREDIT	BALANCE

(The work sheet for this problem is in the back of this booklet.)

GENERAL JOURNAL

DATE	ACCOUNT TITLES AND EXPLANATION	P.R.	DEBIT	CREDIT

DATE	ACCOUNT TITLES AND EXPLANATION	P.R.	DEBIT	CREDIT

(The work sheet for this problem is in the back of this booklet.)

GENERAL JOURNAL

DATE		ACCOUNT TITLES AND EXPLANATION	P.R.	DEBIT	CREDIT

DATE	ACCOUNT TITLES AND EXPLANATION	P.R.	DEBIT	CREDIT

DATE	ACCOUNT TITLES AND EXPLANATION	P.R.	DEBIT	CREDIT

(The work sheet for this problem is in the back of this booklet.)

GENERAL JOURNAL

DATE	ACCOUNT TITLES AND EXPLANATION	P.R.	DEBIT	CREDIT

DATE	ACCOUNT TITLES AND EXPLANATION	P.R.	DEBIT	CREDIT

SALES JOURNAL

PAGE 3

DATE	ACCOUNT DEBITED	INVOICE NUMBER	P.R.	AMOUNT

CASH RECEIPTS JOURNAL

PAGE 3

DATE	ACCOUNT CREDITED	EXPLANATION	P.R.	OTHER ACCOUNTS CREDIT	ACCOUNTS RECEIVABLE CREDIT	SALES CREDIT	SALES DISCOUNTS DEBIT	CASH DEBIT

GENERAL LEDGER

Cash   ACCT. NO. 111

DATE		EXPLANATION	P.R.	DEBIT	CREDIT	BALANCE

Accounts Receivable   ACCT. NO. 112

DATE		EXPLANATION	P.R.	DEBIT	CREDIT	BALANCE

Notes Payable   ACCT. NO. 211

DATE		EXPLANATION	P.R.	DEBIT	CREDIT	BALANCE

Sales   ACCT. NO. 411

DATE		EXPLANATION	P.R.	DEBIT	CREDIT	BALANCE

Sales Discounts   ACCT. NO. 413

DATE		EXPLANATION	P.R.	DEBIT	CREDIT	BALANCE

ACCOUNTS RECEIVABLE LEDGER

NAME   *Mark Loftis*
ADDRESS *1008 High Street*

DATE	EXPLANATION	P.R.	DEBIT	CREDIT	BALANCE

NAME   *Regina Niser*
ADDRESS *1217 Adler Street*

DATE	EXPLANATION	P.R.	DEBIT	CREDIT	BALANCE

NAME   *Helen Stone*
ADDRESS *507 East 10th Street*

DATE	EXPLANATION	P.R.	DEBIT	CREDIT	BALANCE

PAGE 3

PURCHASES JOURNAL

DATE	ACCOUNT CREDITED	DATE OF INVOICE	TERMS	P.R.	ACCOUNTS PAYABLE CREDIT	PURCHASES DEBIT	STORE SUPPLIES DEBIT	OFFICE SUPPLIES DEBIT

PAGE 3

CASH DISBURSEMENTS JOURNAL

DATE	CH. NO.	PAYEE	ACCOUNT DEBITED	P.R.	OTHER ACCOUNTS DEBIT	ACCOUNTS PAYABLE DEBIT	PURCHASES DISCOUNTS CREDIT	CASH CREDIT

GENERAL JOURNAL

DATE	ACCOUNT TITLES AND EXPLANATION	P.R.	DEBIT	CREDIT

GENERAL LEDGER

Cash   ACCT. NO. 111

DATE	EXPLANATION	P.R.	DEBIT	CREDIT	BALANCE

Store Supplies   ACCT. NO. 115

DATE	EXPLANATION	P.R.	DEBIT	CREDIT	BALANCE

Office Supplies   ACCT. NO. 116

DATE	EXPLANATION	P.R.	DEBIT	CREDIT	BALANCE

Store Equipment   ACCT. NO. 131

DATE	EXPLANATION	P.R.	DEBIT	CREDIT	BALANCE

Notes Payable   ACCT. NO. 211

DATE	EXPLANATION	P.R.	DEBIT	CREDIT	BALANCE

Accounts Payable   ACCT. NO. 212

DATE	EXPLANATION	P.R.	DEBIT	CREDIT	BALANCE

Purchases   ACCT. NO. 511

DATE	EXPLANATION	P.R.	DEBIT	CREDIT	BALANCE

Purchases Returns and Allowances   ACCT. NO. 512

DATE	EXPLANATION	P.R.	DEBIT	CREDIT	BALANCE

Purchases Discounts   ACCT. NO. 513

DATE	EXPLANATION	P.R.	DEBIT	CREDIT	BALANCE

Sales Salaries Expense   ACCT. NO. 612

DATE	EXPLANATION	P.R.	DEBIT	CREDIT	BALANCE

		Advertising Expense			ACCT. NO. 61?

DATE		EXPLANATION	P.R.	DEBIT	CREDIT	BALANCE

ACCOUNTS PAYABLE LEDGER

NAME   *Barclay Company*

ADDRESS *Cranston, Illinois*

DATE		EXPLANATION	P.R.	DEBIT	CREDIT	BALANCE

NAME   *Long Company*

ADDRESS *Derby, Ohio*

DATE		EXPLANATION	P.R.	DEBIT	CREDIT	BALANCE

NAME   *Nixen Company*

ADDRESS *Gosport, Indiana*

DATE		EXPLANATION	P.R.	DEBIT	CREDIT	BALANCE

NAME   *Rexor Company*

ADDRESS *32nd and Maple*

DATE		EXPLANATION	P.R.	DEBIT	CREDIT	BALANCE

SALES JOURNAL

PAGE 3

DATE		ACCOUNT DEBITED	INVOICE NUMBER	P.R.	AMOUNT
Jan.	6	Fred Midler	738	√	3 6 4 5 00
	15	Brenda Simms	739	√	4 0 5 0 00
	18	Sam Trent	740	√	3 4 4 5 00

PURCHASES JOURNAL

PAGE 2

DATE		ACCOUNT CREDITED	DATE OF INVOICE	TERMS	P.R.	ACCOUNTS PAYABLE CREDIT	PURCHASES DEBIT	STORE SUPPLIES DEBIT	OFFICE SUPPLIES DEBIT
Jan.	2	Younger Company	1/2	2/10, n/60	√	3 6 0 0 00	3 6 0 0 00		
	5	Reed Suppliers	1/3	n/10 EOM	√	1 6 4 5 00	1 3 5 0 00	2 2 0 00	7 5 00
	17	Younger Company	1/15	2/10, n/60	√	4 4 3 5 00	4 4 3 5 00		
	18	Vax Company	1/16	2/10, n/60	√	2 9 5 0 00	2 9 5 0 00		

CASH RECEIPTS JOURNAL

DATE		ACCOUNT CREDITED	EXPLANATION	P.R.	OTHER ACCOUNTS CREDIT	ACCOUNTS RECEIVABLE CREDIT	SALES CREDIT	SALES DISCOUNTS DEBIT	CASH DEBIT
Jan.	2	Frank Urich	Invoice 12/23	√		4 7 5 0 00		9 5 00	4 6 5 5 00
	15	Sales	Cash sales	√			43 1 5 5 00		43 1 5 5 00
	16	Fred Midler	Invoice 1/6	√		2 7 0 0 00		5 4 00	2 6 4 6 00

CASH DISBURSEMENTS JOURNAL

DATE		CH. NO.	PAYEE	ACCOUNT DEBITED	P.R.	OTHER ACCOUNTS DEBIT	ACCOUNTS PAYABLE DEBIT	PURCHASES DISCOUNT CREDIT	CASH CREDIT
Jan.	2	446	Property Management Co.	Rent Expense	612	2 5 0 0 00			2 5 0 0 00
	6	447	Eclat Company	Eclat Company	√		4 2 5 0 00	8 5 00	4 1 6 5 00
	12	448	Younger Company	Younger Company	√		3 6 0 0 00	7 2 00	3 5 2 8 00
	15	449	Max Davis	Sales Salaries Expense	611	1 4 4 0 00			1 4 4 0 00

GENERAL JOURNAL

DATE		ACCOUNT TITLES AND EXPLANATION	P.R.	DEBIT	CREDIT
Jan.	4	Accounts Payable—Eclat Company	211/√	5 1 5 00	
		Purchases Returns and Allowances	512		5 1 5 00
	9	Sales Returns and Allowances	412	9 4 5 00	
		Accounts Receivable—Fred Midler	112/√		9 4 5 00

ACCOUNTS RECEIVABLE LEDGER

NAME   *Fred Midler*
ADDRESS *1412 West 24th Street*

DATE		EXPLANATION	P.R.	DEBIT	CREDIT	BALANCE
Jan.	6		S3	3 6 4 5 00		3 6 4 5 00
	9		G2		9 4 5 00	2 7 0 0 00
	16		R3		2 7 0 0 00	– 0 –

NAME   *Brenda Simms*
ADDRESS *3434 West 18th Street*

DATE		EXPLANATION	P.R.	DEBIT	CREDIT	BALANCE
Jan.	15		S3	4 0 5 0 00		4 0 5 0 00

NAME   *Sam Trent*
ADDRESS *1412 West 24th Street*

DATE		EXPLANATION	P.R.	DEBIT	CREDIT	BALANCE
Jan.	18		S3	3 4 4 5 00		3 4 4 5 00

NAME   *Frank Urich*
ADDRESS *4314 East Oak Avenue*

DATE		EXPLANATION	P.R.	DEBIT	CREDIT	BALANCE
Dec.	23		S2	4 7 5 0 00		4 7 5 0 00
Jan.	2		R3		4 7 5 0 00	– 0 –

ACCOUNTS PAYABLE LEDGER

NAME   *Eclat Company*
ADDRESS *1010 West 10th Street*

DATE		EXPLANATION	P.R.	DEBIT	CREDIT	BALANCE
Dec.	28		P1		4 7 6 5 00	4 7 6 5 00
Jan.	4		G2	5 1 5 00		4 2 5 0 00
	6		D4	4 2 5 0 00		– 0 –

NAME   *Reed Suppliers*
ADDRESS *711 East 15th Street*

DATE		EXPLANATION	P.R.	DEBIT	CREDIT	BALANCE
Jan.	5		P2		1 6 4 5 00	1 6 4 5 00

NAME   *Vax Company*
ADDRESS *15th and Oak*

DATE		EXPLANATION	P.R.	DEBIT	CREDIT	BALANCE
Jan.	18		P2		2 9 5 0 00	2 9 5 0 00

NAME   *Younger Company*
ADDRESS *4314 East Oak Avenue*

DATE		EXPLANATION	P.R.	DEBIT	CREDIT	BALANCE
Jan.	2		P2		3 600 00	3 600 00
	12		D4	3 600 00		– 0 –
	17		P2		4 435 00	4 435 00

GENERAL LEDGER

Cash   ACCT. NO. *111*

DATE		EXPLANATION	P.R.	DEBIT	CREDIT	BALANCE
Dec.	31	Balance	√			5 895 00

Accounts Receivable   ACCT. NO. *112*

DATE		EXPLANATION	P.R.	DEBIT	CREDIT	BALANCE
Dec.	31	Balance	√			4 750 00
Jan.	9		G2		945 00	3 805 00

Merchandise Inventory   ACCT. NO. *113*

DATE		EXPLANATION	P.R.	DEBIT	CREDIT	BALANCE
Dec.	31	Balance	√			74 420 00

Store Supplies   ACCT. NO. *114*

DATE		EXPLANATION	P.R.	DEBIT	CREDIT	BALANCE
Dec.	31	Balance	√			675 00

Office Supplies   ACCT. NO. 115

DATE		EXPLANATION	P.R.	DEBIT	CREDIT	BALANCE
Dec.	31	Balance	√			3 8 5 00

Store Equipment   ACCT. NO. 131

DATE		EXPLANATION	P.R.	DEBIT	CREDIT	BALANCE
Dec.	31	Balance	√			46 8 1 0 00

Accumulated Depreciation, Store Equipment   ACCT. NO. 132

DATE		EXPLANATION	P.R.	DEBIT	CREDIT	BALANCE
Dec.	31	Balance	√			10 1 7 0 00

Accounts Payable   ACCT. NO. 211

DATE		EXPLANATION	P.R.	DEBIT	CREDIT	BALANCE
Dec.	31	Balance	√			4 7 6 5 00
Jan.	4		G2	5 1 5 00		4 2 5 0 00

Susan Linder, Capital   ACCT. NO. 311

DATE		EXPLANATION	P.R.	DEBIT	CREDIT	BALANCE
Dec.	31	Balance	√			118 0 0 0 00

Susan Linder, Withdrawals   ACCT. NO. 312

DATE		EXPLANATION	P.R.	DEBIT	CREDIT	BALANCE

Sales   ACCT. NO. 411

DATE		EXPLANATION	P.R.	DEBIT	CREDIT	BALANCE

Sales Returns and Allowances   ACCT. NO. 412

DATE		EXPLANATION	P.R.	DEBIT	CREDIT	BALANCE
Jan.	9		G2	9 4 5 00		9 4 5 00

Sales Discounts   ACCT. NO. 413

DATE		EXPLANATION	P.R.	DEBIT	CREDIT	BALANCE

Purchases   ACCT. NO. 511

DATE		EXPLANATION	P.R.	DEBIT	CREDIT	BALANCE

Purchases Returns and Allowances   ACCT. NO. 512

DATE		EXPLANATION	P.R.	DEBIT	CREDIT	BALANCE
Jan.	4		G2		5 1 5 00	5 1 5 00

Purchases Discounts   ACCT. NO. 513

DATE		EXPLANATION	P.R.	DEBIT	CREDIT	BALANCE

Sales Salaries Expense   ACCT. NO. 611

DATE		EXPLANATION	P.R.	DEBIT	CREDIT	BALANCE
Jan.	15		D4	1 4 4 0 00		1 4 4 0 00

Rent Expense   ACCT. NO. 612

DATE		EXPLANATION	P.R.	DEBIT	CREDIT	BALANCE
Jan.	2		D4	2 5 0 0 00		2 5 0 0 00

Utilities Expense   ACCT. NO. 613

DATE		EXPLANATION	P.R.	DEBIT	CREDIT	BALANCE

SALES JOURNAL

PAGE 2

DATE	ACCOUNT DEBITED	INVOICE NUMBER	P.R.	AMOUNT

PURCHASES JOURNAL

PAGE 2

DATE	ACCOUNT CREDITED	DATE OF INVOICE	TERMS	P.R.	ACCOUNTS PAYABLE CREDIT	PURCHASES DEBIT	STORE SUPPLIES DEBIT	OFFICE SUPPLIES DEBIT

CASH RECEIPTS JOURNAL

DATE	ACCOUNT CREDITED	EXPLANATION	P.R.	OTHER ACCOUNTS CREDIT	ACCOUNTS RECEIVABLE CREDIT	SALES CREDIT	SALES DISCOUNTS DEBIT	CASH DEBIT

CASH DISBURSEMENTS JOURNAL

DATE	CH. NO.	PAYEE	ACCOUNT DEBITED	P.R.	OTHER ACCOUNTS DEBIT	ACCOUNTS PAYABLE DEBIT	PURCHASES DISCOUNTS CREDIT	CASH CREDIT

GENERAL JOURNAL

DATE	ACCOUNT TITLES AND EXPLANATION	P.R.	DEBIT	CREDIT

GENERAL LEDGER

Cash

ACCT. NO. 111

DATE	EXPLANATION	P.R.	DEBIT	CREDIT	BALANCE

Accounts Receivable

ACCT. NO. 112

DATE	EXPLANATION	P.R.	DEBIT	CREDIT	BALANCE

Store Supplies

ACCT. NO. 115

DATE	EXPLANATION	P.R.	DEBIT	CREDIT	BALANCE

Office Supplies

ACCT. NO. 116

DATE	EXPLANATION	P.R.	DEBIT	CREDIT	BALANCE

Office Equipment   ACCT. NO. 133

DATE		EXPLANATION	P.R.	DEBIT	CREDIT	BALANCE

Notes Payable   ACCT. NO. 211

DATE		EXPLANATION	P.R.	DEBIT	CREDIT	BALANCE

Accounts Payable   ACCT. NO. 212

DATE		EXPLANATION	P.R.	DEBIT	CREDIT	BALANCE

Sales   ACCT. NO. 411

DATE		EXPLANATION	P.R.	DEBIT	CREDIT	BALANCE

Sales Discounts   ACCT. NO. 413

DATE		EXPLANATION	P.R.	DEBIT	CREDIT	BALANCE

Purchases   ACCT. NO. 511

DATE		EXPLANATION	P.R.	DEBIT	CREDIT	BALANCE

Purchases Returns and Allowances   ACCT. NO. 512

DATE	EXPLANATION	P.R.	DEBIT	CREDIT	BALANCE

Purchases Discounts   ACCT. NO. 513

DATE	EXPLANATION	P.R.	DEBIT	CREDIT	BALANCE

Sales Salaries Expense   ACCT. NO. 612

DATE	EXPLANATION	P.R.	DEBIT	CREDIT	BALANCE

ACCOUNTS RECEIVABLE LEDGER

NAME *Carl Chase*
ADDRESS *4314 East Oak Avenue*

DATE	EXPLANATION	P.R.	DEBIT	CREDIT	BALANCE

NAME *Omar Hanes*
ADDRESS *1412 West 24th Street*

DATE	EXPLANATION	P.R.	DEBIT	CREDIT	BALANCE

NAME   *Leigh Rogers*
ADDRESS *3434 West 18th Street*

DATE	EXPLANATION	P.R.	DEBIT	CREDIT	BALANCE

ACCOUNTS PAYABLE LEDGER

NAME   *Abell Company*
ADDRESS *1212 Ninth Avenue*

DATE	EXPLANATION	P.R.	DEBIT	CREDIT	BALANCE

NAME   *Bradley Company*
ADDRESS *15th and Oak*

DATE	EXPLANATION	P.R.	DEBIT	CREDIT	BALANCE

NAME   *Telecore Company*
ADDRESS *32nd and Maple*

DATE	EXPLANATION	P.R.	DEBIT	CREDIT	BALANCE

NAME   *Thomas Company*
ADDRESS *1412 East Maple Avenue*

DATE	EXPLANATION	P.R.	DEBIT	CREDIT	BALANCE

Name _____

PAGE 3

SALES JOURNAL

DATE	ACCOUNT DEBITED	INVOICE NUMBER	P.R.	AMOUNT

PAGE 3

PURCHASES JOURNAL

DATE	ACCOUNT CREDITED	DATE OF INVOICE	TERMS	P.R.	ACCOUNTS PAYABLE CREDIT	PURCHASES DEBIT	STORE SUPPLIES DEBIT	OFFICE SUPPLIES DEBIT

CASH RECEIPTS JOURNAL

PAGE 3

DATE	ACCOUNT CREDITED	EXPLANATION	P.R.	OTHER ACCOUNTS CREDIT	ACCOUNTS RECEIVABLE CREDIT	SALES CREDIT	SALES DISCOUNTS DEBIT	CASH DEBIT

CASH DISBURSEMENTS JOURNAL

PAGE 3

DATE	CH. NO.	PAYEE	ACCOUNT DEBITED	P.R.	OTHER ACCOUNTS DEBIT	ACCOUNTS PAYABLE DEBIT	PURCHASES DISCOUNTS CREDIT	CASH CREDIT

GENERAL JOURNAL

DATE	ACCOUNT TITLES AND EXPLANATION	P.R.	DEBIT	CREDIT

ACCOUNTS RECEIVABLE LEDGER

NAME   *Kurt Han*
ADDRESS *615 First Street*

DATE	EXPLANATION	P.R.	DEBIT	CREDIT	BALANCE

NAME   *Sheila Jost*
ADDRESS *1316 2nd Avenue North*

DATE	EXPLANATION	P.R.	DEBIT	CREDIT	BALANCE

NAME   *Robert Sunbeck*
ADDRESS *1442 Beck Street*

DATE	EXPLANATION	P.R.	DEBIT	CREDIT	BALANCE

ACCOUNTS PAYABLE LEDGER

NAME   *Barbour Company*
ADDRESS *207 North 22nd Street*

DATE		EXPLANATION	P.R.	DEBIT	CREDIT	BALANCE

NAME   *Elgin Company*
ADDRESS *105 Central Avenue*

DATE		EXPLANATION	P.R.	DEBIT	CREDIT	BALANCE

NAME   *Lakes Company*
ADDRESS *2711 Walnut*

DATE		EXPLANATION	P.R.	DEBIT	CREDIT	BALANCE

NAME   *Outlet Company*
ADDRESS *137 Oak Street*

DATE		EXPLANATION	P.R.	DEBIT	CREDIT	BALANCE

GENERAL LEDGER

Cash   ACCT. NO. *11*

DATE		EXPLANATION	P.R.	DEBIT	CREDIT	BALANCE

Accounts Receivable   ACCT. NO. 112

DATE		EXPLANATION	P.R.	DEBIT	CREDIT	BALANCE

Store Supplies   ACCT. NO. 115

DATE		EXPLANATION	P.R.	DEBIT	CREDIT	BALANCE

Office Supplies   ACCT. NO. 116

DATE		EXPLANATION	P.R.	DEBIT	CREDIT	BALANCE

Store Equipment   ACCT. NO. 131

DATE		EXPLANATION	P.R.	DEBIT	CREDIT	BALANCE

Accounts Payable   ACCT. NO. 212

DATE		EXPLANATION	P.R.	DEBIT	CREDIT	BALANCE

Sales
ACCT. NO. 41

DATE	EXPLANATION	P.R.	DEBIT	CREDIT	BALANCE

Sales Returns and Allowances
ACCT. NO. 41

DATE	EXPLANATION	P.R.	DEBIT	CREDIT	BALANCE

Sales Discounts
ACCT. NO. 41

DATE	EXPLANATION	P.R.	DEBIT	CREDIT	BALANCE

Purchases
ACCT. NO. 51

DATE	EXPLANATION	P.R.	DEBIT	CREDIT	BALANCE

Purchases Returns and Allowances
ACCT. NO. 51

DATE	EXPLANATION	P.R.	DEBIT	CREDIT	BALANCE

Purchases Discounts
ACCT. NO. 51

DATE	EXPLANATION	P.R.	DEBIT	CREDIT	BALANCE

Sales Salaries Expense   ACCT. NO. 612

DATE		EXPLANATION	P.R.	DEBIT	CREDIT	BALANCE

Advertising Expense   ACCT. NO. 615

DATE		EXPLANATION	P.R.	DEBIT	CREDIT	BALANCE

/////

SALES JOURNAL

DATE	ACCOUNT DEBITED	INVOICE NUMBER	P.R.	AMOUNT

PURCHASES JOURNAL

DATE	ACCOUNT CREDITED	DATE OF INVOICE	TERMS	P.R.	ACCOUNTS PAYABLE CREDIT	PURCHASES DEBIT	STORE SUPPLIES DEBIT	OFFICE SUPPLIES DEBIT

CASH RECEIPTS JOURNAL

DATE	ACCOUNT CREDITED	EXPLANATION	P.R.	OTHER ACCOUNTS CREDIT	ACCOUNTS RECEIVABLE CREDIT	SALES CREDIT	SALES DISCOUNTS DEBIT	CASH DEBIT

CASH DISBURSEMENTS JOURNAL

DATE	CH. NO.	PAYEE	ACCOUNT DEBITED	P.R.	OTHER ACCOUNTS DEBIT	ACCOUNTS PAYABLE DEBIT	PURCHASES DISCOUNTS CREDIT	CASH CREDIT

CENTAUR COMPANY (Continued) Name _____

GENERAL JOURNAL

DATE	ACCOUNT TITLES AND EXPLANATION	P.R.	DEBIT	CREDIT

DATE		ACCOUNT TITLES AND EXPLANATION	P.R.	DEBIT	CREDIT

The work sheet for this problem   **GENERAL LEDGER**

s in the back of the book)   *Cash*   ACCT. NO. *111*

DATE		EXPLANATION	P.R.	DEBIT	CREDIT	BALANCE
19— Feb.	28	Balance	√			10 2 7 5 00

Accounts Receivable   ACCT. NO. *112*

DATE		EXPLANATION	P.R.	DEBIT	CREDIT	BALANCE
19— Feb.	28	Balance	√			4 4 2 5 00

Merchandise Inventory   ACCT. NO. *113*

DATE		EXPLANATION	P.R.	DEBIT	CREDIT	BALANCE
19— Feb.	28	Balance	√			41 1 7 5 00

Prepaid Insurance   ACCT. NO. *114*

DATE		EXPLANATION	P.R.	DEBIT	CREDIT	BALANCE
19— Feb.	28	Balance	√			2 0 4 0 00

Store Supplies   ACCT. NO. *115*

DATE		EXPLANATION	P.R.	DEBIT	CREDIT	BALANCE
19— Feb.	28	Balance	√			7 0 5 00

Office Supplies   ACCT. NO. *116*

DATE		EXPLANATION	P.R.	DEBIT	CREDIT	BALANCE
19— Feb.	28	Balance	√			4 3 5 00

Store Equipment   ACCT. NO. 13

DATE		EXPLANATION	P.R.	DEBIT	CREDIT	BALANCE
19— Feb.	28	Balance	√			26 7 0 0 00

Accumulated Depreciation, Store Equipment   ACCT. NO. 13

DATE		EXPLANATION	P.R.	DEBIT	CREDIT	BALANCE
19— Feb.	28	Balance	√			7 3 5 0 00

Office Equipment   ACCT. NO. 13

DATE		EXPLANATION	P.R.	DEBIT	CREDIT	BALANCE
19— Feb.	28	Balance	√			13 8 0 0 00

Accumulated Depreciation, Office Equipment   ACCT. NO. 13

DATE		EXPLANATION	P.R.	DEBIT	CREDIT	BALANCE
19— Feb.	28	Balance	√			4 8 0 0 00

Accounts Payable   ACCT. NO. 21

DATE		EXPLANATION	P.R.	DEBIT	CREDIT	BALANCE
19— Feb.	28	Balance	√			3 5 4 0 00

Henry Sutton, Capital   ACCT. NO. 31

DATE		EXPLANATION	P.R.	DEBIT	CREDIT	BALANCE
19— Feb.	28	Balance	√			83 8 6 5 00

Henry Sutton, Withdrawals　　　　ACCT. NO. 312

DATE		EXPLANATION	P.R.	DEBIT	CREDIT	BALANCE

Income Summary　　　　ACCT. NO. 313

DATE		EXPLANATION	P.R.	DEBIT	CREDIT	BALANCE

Sales　　　　ACCT. NO. 411

DATE		EXPLANATION	P.R.	DEBIT	CREDIT	BALANCE

Sales Returns and Allowances　　　　ACCT. NO. 412

DATE		EXPLANATION	P.R.	DEBIT	CREDIT	BALANCE

Sales Discounts　　　　ACCT. NO. 413

DATE		EXPLANATION	P.R.	DEBIT	CREDIT	BALANCE

Purchases　　　　ACCT. NO. 511

DATE		EXPLANATION	P.R.	DEBIT	CREDIT	BALANCE

Purchases Returns and Allowances   ACCT. NO. 512

DATE	EXPLANATION	P.R.	DEBIT	CREDIT	BALANCE

Purchases Discounts   ACCT. NO. 513

DATE	EXPLANATION	P.R.	DEBIT	CREDIT	BALANCE

Sales Salaries Expense   ACCT. NO. 611

DATE	EXPLANATION	P.R.	DEBIT	CREDIT	BALANCE

Rent Expense, Selling Space   ACCT. NO. 612

DATE	EXPLANATION	P.R.	DEBIT	CREDIT	BALANCE

Store Supplies Expense   ACCT. NO. 613

DATE	EXPLANATION	P.R.	DEBIT	CREDIT	BALANCE

Depreciation Expense, Store Equipment   ACCT. NO. 614

DATE	EXPLANATION	P.R.	DEBIT	CREDIT	BALANCE

Office Salaries Expense   ACCT. NO. 651

DATE		EXPLANATION	P.R.	DEBIT	CREDIT	BALANCE

Rent Expense, Office Space   ACCT. NO. 652

DATE		EXPLANATION	P.R.	DEBIT	CREDIT	BALANCE

Insurance Expense   ACCT. NO. 653

DATE		EXPLANATION	P.R.	DEBIT	CREDIT	BALANCE

Office Supplies Expense   ACCT. NO. 654

DATE		EXPLANATION	P.R.	DEBIT	CREDIT	BALANCE

Depreciation Expense, Office Equipment   ACCT. NO. 655

DATE		EXPLANATION	P.R.	DEBIT	CREDIT	BALANCE

Utilities Expense   ACCT. NO. 656

DATE		EXPLANATION	P.R.	DEBIT	CREDIT	BALANCE

ACCOUNTS RECEIVABLE LEDGER

NAME   *Anchor Company*
ADDRESS *1212 North Bay*

DATE		EXPLANATION	P.R.	DEBIT	CREDIT	BALANCE

NAME   *Blutex Company*
ADDRESS *2000 Industry Road*

DATE		EXPLANATION	P.R.	DEBIT	CREDIT	BALANCE
19– Feb.	28		S2	4 4 2 5 00		4 4 2 5 00

NAME   *Maxwell Constructors*
ADDRESS *407 North 15th Street*

DATE		EXPLANATION	P.R.	DEBIT	CREDIT	BALANCE

NAME   *Pete's Repairs*
ADDRESS *124 Washington Avenue*

DATE		EXPLANATION	P.R.	DEBIT	CREDIT	BALANCE

ACCOUNTS PAYABLE LEDGER

NAME   *Hardman Products*
ADDRESS *7300 Falcon Ledge*

DATE		EXPLANATION	P.R.	DEBIT	CREDIT	BALANCE
19– Feb.	27		P1		3 5 4 0 00	3 5 4 0 00

NAME   *Reston Suppliers*
ADDRESS *13 Oakdale*

DATE		EXPLANATION	P.R.	DEBIT	CREDIT	BALANCE

NAME   *Thomas Brothers*
ADDRESS *1212 Castle Ridge*

DATE		EXPLANATION	P.R.	DEBIT	CREDIT	BALANCE

NAME   *Worth Materials*
ADDRESS *725 St. John's Boulevard*

DATE		EXPLANATION	P.R.	DEBIT	CREDIT	BALANCE

CENTAUR COMPANY

Income Statement

For the Month Ended March 31, 19--

CENTAUR COMPANY
Statement of Changes in Owner's Equity
For the Month Ended March 31, 19--

CENTAUR COMPANY
Balance Sheet
March 31, 19--

CENTAUR COMPANY

Post-closing Trial Balance

March 31, 19--

CENTAUR COMPANY

Schedule of Accounts Receivable

March 31, 19--

CENTAUR COMPANY

Schedule of Accounts Payable

March 31, 19--

Part 1

GENERAL JOURNAL

DATE	ACCOUNT TITLES AND EXPLANATION	P.R.	DEBIT	CREDIT

Part 2

DATE		ACCOUNT TITLES AND EXPLANATION	P.R.	DEBIT	CREDIT

Part 1

GENERAL JOURNAL

DATE	ACCOUNT TITLES AND EXPLANATION	P.R.	DEBIT	CREDIT

Part 2

Part 3

DATE		ACCOUNT TITLES AND EXPLANATION	P.R.	DEBIT	CREDIT

Part 1

DATE		ACCOUNT TITLES AND EXPLANATION	P.R.	DEBIT	CREDIT

GENERAL JOURNAL

DATE		ACCOUNT TITLES AND EXPLANATION	P.R.	DEBIT	CREDIT

DATE	ACCOUNT TITLES AND EXPLANATION	P.R.	DEBIT	CREDIT

Part 1, (a)   **GENERAL JOURNAL**

DATE	ACCOUNT TITLES AND EXPLANATION	P.R.	DEBIT	CREDIT

Part 2, (a)

DATE	ACCOUNT TITLES AND EXPLANATION	P.R.	DEBIT	CREDIT

Part 2, (b)

Voucher

	DATE	VCHR. NO.	PAYEE	WHEN AND HOW PAID		VOUCHERS PAYABLE CREDIT	PURCHASES DEBIT	TRANSPORTA-TION-IN DEBIT	
				DATE	CH. NO.				
1									1
2									2
3									3
4									4
5									5
6									6
7									7
8									8
9									9
10									10

Register   PAGE 5

	SALES SALARIES EXPENSE DEBIT	ADVER-TISING EXPENSE DEBIT	OFFICE SALARIES EXPENSE DEBIT	OTHER ACCOUNTS DEBIT			
				ACCOUNT NAME	P.R.	AMOUNT	
1							1
2							2
3							3
4							4
5							5
6							6
7							7
8							8
9							9
10							10

Check Register   PAGE 5

DATE	PAYEE	VCHR. NO.	CH. NO.	VOUCHERS PAYABLE DR.	PURCHASES DISCOUNT CR.	CASH CR.

GENERAL JOURNAL

DATE	ACCOUNT TITLES AND EXPLANATION	P.R.	DEBIT	CREDIT

Vouchers Payable

ACCT. No. 212

DATE	EXPLANATION	P.R.	DEBIT	CREDIT	BALANCE

VOUCHER NUMBER	PAYEE	AMOUNT

Part 1   **GENERAL JOURNAL**

DATE	ACCOUNT TITLES AND EXPLANATION	P.R.	DEBIT	CREDIT

DATE	ACCOUNT TITLES AND EXPLANATION	P.R.	DEBIT	CREDIT

Part 2

Part 3

GENERAL JOURNAL

DATE	ACCOUNT TITLES AND EXPLANATION	P.R.	DEBIT	CREDIT

GENERAL JOURNAL

DATE	ACCOUNT TITLES AND EXPLANATION	P.R.	DEBIT	CREDIT

DATE	ACCOUNT TITLES AND EXPLANATION	P.R.	DEBIT	CREDIT

GENERAL JOURNAL

DATE	ACCOUNT TITLES AND EXPLANATION	P.R.	DEBIT	CREDIT

Part 2

Part 3

Part 1

Part 2

GENERAL JOURNAL

DATE	ACCOUNT TITLES AND EXPLANATION	P.R.	DEBIT	CREDIT

Part 3

GENERAL JOURNAL

DATE	ACCOUNT TITLES AND EXPLANATION	P.R.	DEBIT	CREDIT

DATE		ACCOUNT TITLES AND EXPLANATION	P.R.	DEBIT	CREDIT

GENERAL JOURNAL

DATE	ACCOUNT TITLES AND EXPLANATION	P.R.	DEBIT	CREDIT

DATE		ACCOUNT TITLES AND EXPLANATION	P.R.	DEBIT	CREDIT

GENERAL JOURNAL

DATE	ACCOUNT TITLES AND EXPLANATION	P.R.	DEBIT	CREDIT

DATE	ACCOUNT TITLES AND EXPLANATION	P.R.	DEBIT	CREDIT

	FIFO			LIFO			WEIGHTED-AVERAGE COST		
Sales									
Cost of goods sold:									
Inventory, January 1, 1990									
Purchases									
Goods available for sale									
Inventory, December 31, 1990									
Cost of goods sold									
Gross profit on sales									
Operating expenses									
Net income									

Case 1

Product	Units on Hand	Per Unit Cost	Per Unit Market	Total Cost	Total Market	Lower of Cost or Market (by product)

Case 2

Product	Units on Hand	Per Unit Cost	Per Unit Market	Total Cost	Total Market	Lower of Cost or Market (by product)

Case 3

Product	Units on Hand	Per Unit		Total Cost	Total Market	Lower of Cost or Market (by product)
		Cost	Market			

Part 1

	1989	1990	1991

Part 2

Part 1

Item _____ Location in stockroom _____

Maximum _____ Minimum _____

DATE		PURCHASED					SOLD					BALANCE			
		UNITS	COST		TOTAL		UNITS	COST		TOTAL		UNITS	COST		BALANCE	

Part 2

Item_____   Location in stockroom _____

Maximum _____ Minimum_____

DATE	PURCHASED			SOLD			BALANCE		
	UNITS	COST	TOTAL	UNITS	COST	TOTAL	UNITS	COST	BALANCE

Part 3

DATE	ACCOUNT TITLES AND EXPLANATION	P.R.	DEBIT	CREDIT

Part 1

Year	Straight Line	Units of Production	Declining Balance	Sum-of-the-Years' Digits

Part 2   GENERAL JOURNAL

DATE		ACCOUNT TITLES AND EXPLANATION	P.R.	DEBIT	CREDIT

Plant Equipment

DATE	EXPLANATION	P.R.	DEBIT	CREDIT	BALANCE

Accumulated Depreciation, Plant Equipment

DATE	EXPLANATION	P.R.	DEBIT	CREDIT	BALANCE

SUBSIDIARY PLANT ASSET AND DEPRECIATION RECORD No. _____

Item _____

Mfg. Serial No. _____

Estimated Life _____

Depreciation per year _____

General Ledger
Account _____

Purchased
from _____

Estimated Salvage Value _____

per month _____

		Asset Record			Depreciation Record		
Date	Explanation	Debit	Credit	Balance	Debit	Credit	Balance

Final Disposition of the Asset _____

SUBSIDIARY PLANT ASSET AND DEPRECIATION RECORD No. _____

Item _____

Mfg. Serial No. _____

Estimated Life _____

Depreciation per year _____

General Ledger
Account _____

Purchased
from _____

Estimated Salvage Value _____

per month _____

		Asset Record			Depreciation Record		
Date	Explanation	Debit	Credit	Balance	Debit	Credit	Balance

Final Disposition of the Asset _____

SUBSIDIARY PLANT ASSET AND DEPRECIATION RECORD No. _____

Item _____   General Ledger
Account _____

Mfg. Serial No. _____   Purchased
from _____

Estimated Life _____   Estimated Salvage Value _____

Depreciation per year _____   per month _____

Date	Explanation	Asset Record			Depreciation Record		
		Debit	Credit	Balance	Debit	Credit	Balance

Final Disposition of the Asset _____

Part 1

	Land	Building _____	Building _____	Land Improvements _____	Land Improvements _____

Parts 2 and 3

DATE	ACCOUNT TITLES AND EXPLANATION	P.R.	DEBIT	CREDIT

DATE	ACCOUNT TITLES AND EXPLANATION	P.R.	DEBIT	CREDIT

Machine Number	1988 Depreciation	1989 Depreciation	1990 Depreciation	1991 Depreciation	1992 Depreciation

GENERAL JOURNAL

DATE	ACCOUNT TITLES AND EXPLANATION	P.R.	DEBIT	CREDIT

DATE	ACCOUNT TITLES AND EXPLANATION	P.R.	DEBIT	CREDIT

GENERAL JOURNAL

DATE	ACCOUNT TITLES AND EXPLANATION	P.R.	DEBIT	CREDIT

GENERAL JOURNAL

DATE	ACCOUNT TITLES AND EXPLANATION	P.R.	DEBIT	CREDIT

Part 1

DATE		ACCOUNT TITLES AND EXPLANATION	P.R.	DEBIT	CREDIT

Part 2

DATE		ACCOUNT TITLES AND EXPLANATION	P.R.	DEBIT	CREDIT

Part 1   **GENERAL JOURNAL**

DATE	ACCOUNT TITLES AND EXPLANATION	P.R.	DEBIT	CREDIT

Part 2   GENERAL JOURNAL

DATE	ACCOUNT TITLES AND EXPLANATION	P.R.	DEBIT	CREDIT

Part 1   GENERAL JOURNAL

DATE	ACCOUNT TITLES AND EXPLANATION	P.R.	DEBIT	CREDIT

Part 2

DATE		ACCOUNT TITLES AND EXPLANATION	P.R.	DEBIT	CREDIT

GENERAL JOURNAL

DATE	ACCOUNT TITLES AND EXPLANATION	P.R.	DEBIT	CREDIT

DATE	ACCOUNT TITLES AND EXPLANATION	P.R.	DEBIT	CREDIT

Part 1

Year	(a) Face Amount of Note	(b) Unamortized Discount at Beginning of Year	(c) Beginning-of-Year Carrying Amount (a) − (b)	(d) Discount to Be Amortized Each Year (c) × %	(e) Unamortized Discount at End of Year (b) − (d)	(f) End-of-Year Carring Amount (a) − (e)

Part 2

DATE	ACCOUNT TITLES AND EXPLANATION	P.R.	DEBIT	CREDIT

Part 1

Year	Beginning-of-Year Lease Liability	Beginning-of-Year Unamortized Discount	Beginning-of-Year Carrying Amount	Discount to be Amortized	Unamortized Discount at End of Year	End-of-Year Lease Liability	End-of-Year Carrying Amount

Part 2

Parts 3, 4, and 5

DATE	ACCOUNT TITLES AND EXPLANATION	P.R.	DEBIT	CREDIT

Parts 1, 2, and 3

DATE	ACCOUNT TITLES AND EXPLANATION	P.R.	DEBIT	CREDIT

Part 4

Year	Beginning-of-Year Lease Liability	Beginning-of-Year Unamortized Discount	Beginning-of-Year Carrying Amount	Discount to be Amortized	Unamortized Discount at End of Year	End-of-Year Lease Liability	End-of-Year Carrying Amount

CAMPBELL STOOP COMPANY

Work Sheet

For Year Ended December 31, 1990

Part 1

ACCOUNT TITLES	UNADJUSTED TRIAL BALANCE		ADJUSTMENTS		INCOME STATEMENT		ST. OF CH. IN O.E. OR BALANCE SHEET	
	DR.	CR.	DR.	CR.	DR.	CR.	DR.	CR.
Cash								
Accounts receivable								
Allow. for doubtful accts.								
Merchandise inventory								
Equipment								
Accum. depr., equipment								
Building								
Accum. depr., building								
Patents								
Accounts payable								
Est. warranty liability								
Interest payable								
Notes payable								
Bill Campbell, capital								
Bill Campbell, withdrawals								
Sales								
Interest earned								
Purchases								
Depr. expense, equipment								
Depr. expense, building								
Wages expense								
Bad debts expense								
Patents amort. expense								
Legal expense								
Warranty expense								
Interest expense								
Miscellaneous expense								

Part 2

GENERAL JOURNAL

DATE	ACCOUNT TITLES AND EXPLANATION	P.R.	DEBIT	CREDIT

Part 3

DATE	ACCOUNT TITLES AND EXPLANATION	P.R.	DEBIT	CREDIT

CAMPBELL STOOP COMPANY

Income Statement

For Year Ended December 31, 1990

CAMPBELL STOOP COMPANY

Statement of Changes in Owner's Equity

For Year Ended December 31, 1990

CAMPBELL STOOP COMPANY

Balance Sheet

December 31, 1990

GENERAL JOURNAL

DATE	ACCOUNT TITLES AND EXPLANATION	P.R.	DEBIT	CREDIT

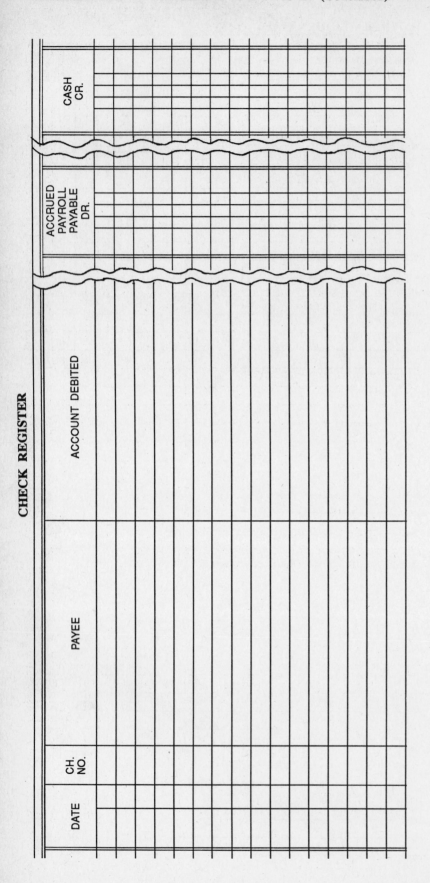

CHECK REGISTER

GENERAL JOURNAL

DATE	ACCOUNT TITLES AND EXPLANATION	P.R.	DEBIT	CREDIT

PAYROLL REGISTER

EMPLOYEE	CLOCK CARD NUMBER	DAILY TIME							TOTAL HOURS	O.T. HOURS	REG. PAY RATE	EARNINGS			
		M	T	W	T	F	S	S				REGULAR PAY	O.T. PREMIUM PAY	GROSS PAY	
															1
															2
															3
															4
															5
															6
															7
															8
															9

CHECK REGISTER

DATE	CH. No.	PAYEE	ACCOUNT DEBITED	
				1
				2
				3
				4
				5
				6
				7
				8

Week ended

	FICA TAXES		INCOME TAXES		MEDICAL INSUR-ANCE		UNION DUES		TOTAL DEDUC-TIONS		NET PAY		CHECK NUMBER	OFFICE SALARIES EXPENSE		PLANT SALARIES EXPENSE		SERVICE WAGES EXPENSE	
	DEDUCTIONS										PAYMENT				DISTRIBUTION				
1																			
2																			
3																			
4																			
5																			
6																			
7																			
8																			
9																			

	P.R.	OTHER ACCOUNTS DR.			ACCOUNTS PAYABLE DR.			ACCRUED PAYROLL PAYABLE DR.			PURCHASES DISCOUNT CR.			CASH CR.		
1																
2																
3																
4																
5																
6																
7																
8																

GENERAL JOURNAL

DATE	ACCOUNT TITLES AND EXPLANATION	P.R.	DEBIT	CREDIT

DATE	ACCOUNT TITLES AND EXPLANATION	P.R.	DEBIT	CREDIT

PAYROLL REGISTER

EMPLOYEE	CLOCK CARD NUMBER	DAILY TIME							TOTAL HOURS	O.T. HOURS	REG. PAY RATE	EARNINGS			
		M	T	W	T	F	S	S				REGULAR PAY	O.T. PREMIUM PAY	GROSS PAY	
															1
															2
															3
															4
															5
															6
															7
															8
															9

CHECK REGISTER

DATE	CH. NO.	PAYEE	ACCOUNT DEBITED	
				1
				2
				3
				4
				5
				6
				7
				8

Week ended

	DEDUCTIONS					PAYMENT		DISTRIBUTION		
	FICA TAXES	INCOME TAXES	MEDICAL INSUR-ANCE	UNION DUES	TOTAL DEDUC-TIONS	NET PAY	CHECK NUMBER	SALES SALARIES	OFFICE SALARIES	SHOP WAGES
1										
2										
3										
4										
5										
6										
7										
8										
9										

	P.R.	OTHER ACCOUNTS DR.	ACCOUNTS PAYABLE DR.	ACCRUED PAYROLL PAYABLE DR.	PURCHASES DISCOUNT CR.	CASH CR.
1						
2						
3						
4						
5						
6						
7						
8						

GENERAL JOURNAL

DATE	ACCOUNT TITLES AND EXPLANATION	P.R.	DEBIT	CREDIT

CHECK REGISTER

DATE	CH. NO.	PAYEE	ACCOUNT DEBITED	P.R.	OTHER ACCOUNTS DR.	ACCRUED PAYROLL PAYABLE DR.	CASH CR.

GENERAL JOURNAL

DATE	ACCOUNT TITLES AND EXPLANATION	P.R.	DEBIT	CREDIT

DATE	ACCOUNT TITLES AND EXPLANATION	P.R.	DEBIT	CREDIT

Inc./Loss Sharing Plan	Year _____ Calculations				

Inc./Loss Sharing Plan	Year _____		
	Calculations		

Inc./Loss Sharing Plan	Year _____ Calculations				

Part 1

Inc./Loss Sharing Plan	Calculations								

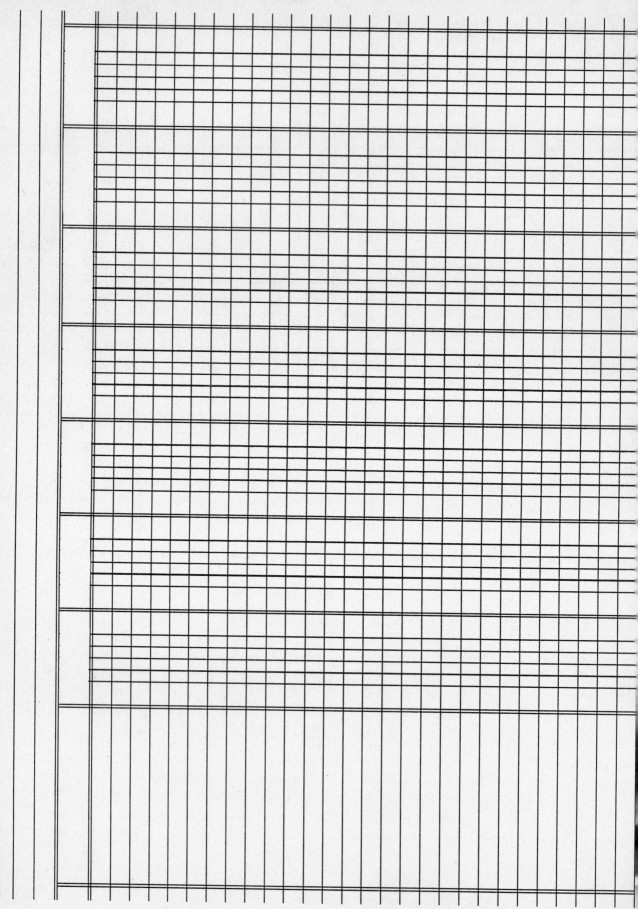

Part 2

Part 3   **GENERAL JOURNAL**

DATE	ACCOUNT TITLES AND EXPLANATION	P.R.	DEBIT	CREDIT

GENERAL JOURNAL

DATE	ACCOUNT TITLES AND EXPLANATION	P.R.	DEBIT	CREDIT

DATE	ACCOUNT TITLES AND EXPLANATION	P.R.	DEBIT	CREDIT

GENERAL JOURNAL

DATE	ACCOUNT TITLES AND EXPLANATION	P.R.	DEBIT	CREDIT

GENERAL JOURNAL

DATE	ACCOUNT TITLES AND EXPLANATION	P.R.	DEBIT	CREDIT

GENERAL JOURNAL

DATE	ACCOUNT TITLES AND EXPLANATION	P.R.	DEBIT	CREDIT

GENERAL JOURNAL

DATE	ACCOUNT TITLES AND EXPLANATION	P.R.	DEBIT	CREDIT

GENERAL JOURNAL

DATE	ACCOUNT TITLES AND EXPLANATION	P.R.	DEBIT	CREDIT

DATE	ACCOUNT TITLES AND EXPLANATION	P.R.	DEBIT	CREDIT

DATE	ACCOUNT TITLES AND EXPLANATION	P.R.	DEBIT	CREDIT

Assignment _____   Name _____

323

Assignment _____   Name _____

Assignment _____   Name _____

331

ACCOUNT TITLES	TRIAL BALANCE		ADJUSTMENTS		ADJUSTED TRIAL BALANCE		INCOME STATEMENT		RETAINED EARNINGS STATEMENT OR BALANCE SHEET	
	DR.	CR.	DR.	CR.	DR.	CR.	DR.	CR.	DR.	CR.

ACCOUNT TITLES	TRIAL BALANCE		ADJUSTMENTS		ADJUSTED TRIAL BALANCE		INCOME STATEMENT		ST. OF CH. IN O. E. OR BALANCE SHEET	
	DR.	CR.	DR.	CR.	DR.	CR.	DR.	CR.	DR.	CR.